MAXnotes®

William Shakespeare's

As You Like It

Text by
Michael Morrison
(Ph.D., CUNY)
Department of English
DeVry Institute
Woodbridge, New Jersey

Illustrations by
Thomas E. Cantillon

Research & Education Association

MAXnotes® for
AS YOU LIKE IT

Copyright © 1996 by Research & Education
Association. All rights reserved. No part of this
book may be reproduced in any form without
permission of the publisher.

Printed in the United States of America

Library of Congress Catalog Card Number 96-67405

International Standard Book Number 0-87891-003-4

MAXnotes® is a registered trademark of
Research & Education Association, Piscataway, New Jersey 08854

What **MAXnotes®** Will Do for You

This book is intended to help you absorb the essential contents and features of William Shakespeare's *As You Like It* and to help you gain a thorough understanding of the work. The book has been designed to do this more quickly and effectively than any other study guide.

For best results, this **MAXnotes** book should be used as a companion to the actual work, not instead of it. The interaction between the two will greatly benefit you.

To help you in your studies, this book presents the most up-to-date interpretations of every section of the actual work, followed by questions and fully explained answers that will enable you to analyze the material critically. The questions also will help you to test your understanding of the work and will prepare you for discussions and exams.

Meaningful illustrations are included to further enhance your understanding and enjoyment of the literary work. The illustrations are designed to place you into the mood and spirit of the work's settings.

The **MAXnotes** also include summaries, character lists, explanations of plot, and section-by-section analyses. A biography of the author and discussion of the work's historical context will help you put this literary piece into the proper perspective of what is taking place.

The use of this study guide will save you the hours of preparation time that would ordinarily be required to arrive at a complete grasp of this work of literature. You will be well prepared for classroom discussions, homework, and exams. The guidelines that are included for writing papers and reports on various topics will prepare you for any added work which may be assigned.

The **MAXnotes** will take your grades "to the max."

Dr. Max Fogiel
Program Director

Contents

> **Each Scene includes List of Characters,
> Summary, Analysis, Study Questions and
> Answers, and Suggested Essay Topics.**

SECTION ONE

Introduction

The Life and Work of William Shakespeare

The details of William Shakespeare's life are sketchy, mostly mere surmise based upon court or other clerical records. His parents, John and Mary (Arden), were married about 1557; she was of the landed gentry, and he was a yeoman—a glover and commodities merchant. By 1568, John had risen through the ranks of town government and held the position of high bailiff, which was a position similar to mayor. William, the eldest son and the third of eight children, was born in 1564, probably on April 23, several days before his baptism on April 26 in Stratford-upon-Avon. Shakespeare is also believed to have died on the same date—April 23—in 1616.

It is believed that William attended the local grammar school in Stratford where his parents lived, and that he studied primarily Latin, rhetoric, logic, and literature. Shakespeare probably left school at age 15, which was the norm, to take a job, especially since this was the period of his father's financial difficulty. At age 18 (1582), William married Anne Hathaway, a local farmer's daughter who was eight years his senior. Their first daughter (Susanna) was born six months later (1583), and twins Judith and Hamnet were born in 1585.

Shakespeare's life can be divided into three periods: the first 20 years in Stratford, which include his schooling, early marriage, and fatherhood; the next 25 years as an actor and playwright in London; and the last five in retirement in Stratford where he enjoyed moderate wealth gained from his theatrical successes. The years linking the first two periods are marked by a lack of information about Shakespeare, and are often referred to as the "dark years."

At some point during the "dark years," Shakespeare began his career with a London theatrical company, perhaps in 1589, for he was already an actor and playwright of some note by 1592. Shakespeare apparently wrote and acted for numerous theatrical companies, including Pembroke's Men, and Strange's Men, which later became the Chamberlain's Men, with whom he remained for the rest of his career.

In 1592, the Plague closed the theaters for about two years, and Shakespeare turned to writing book-length narrative poetry. Most notable were *Venus and Adonis* and *The Rape of Lucrece*, both of which were dedicated to the Earl of Southampton, whom scholars accept as Shakespeare's friend and benefactor despite a lack of documentation. During this same period, Shakespeare was writing his sonnets, which are more likely signs of the time's fashion rather than actual love poems detailing any particular relationship. He returned to playwriting when theaters reopened in 1594, and did not continue to write poetry. His sonnets were published without his consent in 1609, shortly before his retirement.

Amid all of his success, Shakespeare suffered the loss of his only son, Hamnet, who died in 1596 at the age of 11. But Shakespeare's career continued unabated, and in London in 1599, he became one of the partners in the new Globe Theater, which was built by the Chamberlain's Men.

Shakespeare wrote very little after 1612, which was the year he completed *Henry VIII*. It was during a performance of this play in 1613 that the Globe caught fire and burned to the ground. Sometime between 1610 and 1613, Shakespeare returned to Stratford, where he owned a large house and property, to spend his remaining years with his family.

William Shakespeare died on April 23, 1616, and was buried two days later in the chancel of Holy Trinity Church, where he had been baptized exactly 52 years earlier. His literary legacy included 37 plays, 154 sonnets, and five major poems.

Incredibly, most of Shakespeare's plays had never been published in anything except pamphlet form, and were simply extant as acting scripts stored at the Globe. Theater scripts were not regarded as literary works of art, but only the basis for the performance. Plays were simply a popular form of entertainment for all layers of society in Shakespeare's time. Only the efforts of two of Shakespeare's company, John Heminges and Henry Condell, preserved his 36 plays (minus *Pericles*, the thirty-seventh).

Shakespeare's Language

Shakespeare's language can create a strong pang of intimidation, even fear, in a large number of modern-day readers. Fortunately, however, this need not be the case. All that is needed to master the art of reading Shakespeare is to practice the techniques of unraveling uncommonly-structured sentences and to become familiar with the poetic use of uncommon words. We must realize that during the 400-year span between Shakespeare's time and our own, both the way we live and speak has changed. Although most of his vocabulary is in use today, some of it is obsolete, and what may be most confusing is that some of his words are used today, but with slightly different or totally different meanings. On the stage, actors readily dissolve these language stumbling blocks. They study Shakespeare's dialogue and express it dramatically in word and in action so that its meaning is graphically enacted. If the reader studies Shakespeare's lines as an actor does, looking up and reflecting upon the meaning of unfamiliar words until the real voice is discovered, he or she will suddenly experience the excitement, the depth, and the sheer poetry of what these characters say.

Shakespeare's Sentences

In English, or any other language, the meaning of a sentence greatly depends upon where each word is placed in that sentence. "The child hurt the mother" and "The mother hurt the child" have opposite meanings, even though the words are the same, simply because the words are arranged differently. Because word position is so integral to English, the reader will find unfamiliar word arrangements confusing, even difficult to understand. Since Shakespeare's plays are poetic dramas, he often shifts from average word arrangements to the strikingly unusual so that the line will conform to the desired poetic rhythm. Often, too, Shakespeare employs unusual word order to afford a character his own specific style of speaking.

Today, English sentence structure follows a sequence of subject first, verb second, and an optional object third. Shakespeare, however, often places the verb before the subject, which reads, "Speaks he" rather than "He speaks." Solanio speaks with this inverted structure in *The Merchant of Venice* stating, "I should be still/ Plucking the grass to know where sits the wind" (Bevington edition, I, i, ll.17-19), while today's standard English word order would have the clause at the end of this line read, "where the wind sits." "Wind" is the subject of this clause, and "sits" is the verb. Bassanio's words in Act Two also exemplify this inversion: "And in such eyes as ours appear not faults" (II, ii, l. 184). In our normal word order, we would say, "Faults do not appear in eyes such as ours," with "faults" as the subject in both Shakespeare's word order and ours.

Inversions like these are not troublesome, but when Shakespeare positions the predicate adjective or the object before the subject and verb, we are sometimes surprised. For example, rather than "I saw him," Shakespeare may use a structure such as "Him I saw." Similarly, "Cold the morning is" would be used for our "The morning is cold." Lady Macbeth demonstrates this inversion as she speaks of her husband: "Glamis thou art, and Cawdor, and shalt be/What thou art promised" (*Macbeth*, I, v, ll. 14-15). In current English word order, this quote would begin, "Thou art Glamis, and Cawdor."

In addition to inversions, Shakespeare purposefully keeps words apart that we generally keep together. To illustrate, consider Bassanio's humble admission in *The Merchant of Venice*: "I owe you much, and, like a wilful youth,/That which I owe is lost" (I, i, ll. 146-147). The phrase, "like a wilful youth," separates the regular sequence of "I owe you much" and "That which I owe is lost." To understand more clearly this type of passage, the reader could rearrange these word groups into our conventional order: I owe you much and I wasted what you gave me because I was young and impulsive. While these rearranged clauses will sound like normal English, and will be simpler to understand, they will no longer have the desired poetic rhythm, and the emphasis will now be on the wrong words.

As we read Shakespeare, we will find words that are separated by long, interruptive statements. Often subjects are separated from verbs, and verbs are separated from objects. These long interruptions can be used to give a character dimension or to add an element of suspense. For example, in *Romeo and Juliet*, Benvolio describes both Romeo's moodiness and his own sensitive and thoughtful nature:

> I, measuring his affections by my own,
> Which then most sought, where most might not be found,
> Being one too many by my weary self,
> Pursu'd my humour, not pursuing his,
> And gladly shunn'd who gladly fled from me.
> (I, i, ll. 126-130)

In this passage, the subject "I" is distanced from its verb "Pursu'd." The long interruption serves to provide information which is integral to the plot. Another example, taken from *Hamlet*, is the ghost, Hamlet's father, who describes Hamlet's uncle, Claudius, as

> ...that incestuous, that adulterate beast,
> With witchcraft of his wit, with traitorous gifts—
> O wicked wit and gifts, that have the power
> So to seduce—won to his shameful lust
> The will of my most seeming virtuous queen.
> (I, v, ll. 43-47)

From this we learn that Prince Hamlet's mother is the victim of an evil seduction and deception. The delay between the subject, "beast," and the verb, "won," creates a moment of tension filled with the image of a cunning predator waiting for the right moment to spring into attack. This interruptive passage allows the play to unfold crucial information and thus to build the tension necessary to produce a riveting drama.

While at times these long delays are merely for decorative purposes, they are often used to narrate a particular situation or to enhance character development. As *Antony and Cleopatra* opens, an interruptive passage occurs in the first few lines. Although the delay is not lengthy, Philo's words vividly portray Antony's military prowess while they also reveal the immediate concern of the drama.

Antony is distracted from his career and is now focused on Cleopatra:

> ...those goodly eyes,
> That o'er the files and musters of the war
> Have glow'd like plated Mars, now bend, now turn
> The office and devotion of their view
> Upon a tawny front.... (I, i, ll. 2-6)

Whereas Shakespeare sometimes heaps detail upon detail, his sentences are often elliptical, that is, they omit words we expect in written English sentences. In fact, we often do this in our spoken conversations. For instance, we say, "You see that?" when we really mean, "Did you see that?" Reading poetry or listening to lyrics in music conditions us to supply the omitted words and it makes us more comfortable reading this type of dialogue. Consider one passage in *The Merchant of Venice* where Antonio's friends ask him why he seems so sad and Solanio tells Antonio, "Why, then you are in love" (I, i, l. 46). When Antonio denies this, Solanio responds, "Not in love neither?" (I, i, l. 47). The word "you" is omitted but understood despite the confusing double negative.

In addition to leaving out words, Shakespeare often uses intentionally vague language, a strategy which taxes the reader's attentiveness. In *Antony and Cleopatra*, Cleopatra, upset that Antony is leaving for Rome after learning that his wife died in battle, convinces him to stay in Egypt:

> Sir, you and I must part, but that's not it:
> Sir you and I have lov'd, but there's not it;
> That you know well, something it is I would—
> O, my oblivion is a very Antony,
> And I am all forgotten.
> (I, iii, ll. 87-91, emphasis added)

In line 89, "...something it is I would" suggests that there is something that she would want to say, do, or have done. The intentional vagueness leaves us, and certainly Antony, to wonder. Though this sort of writing may appear lackadaisical for all that it leaves out, here the vagueness functions to portray Cleopatra as rhetorically sophisticated. Similarly, when asked what thing a crocodile is (meaning Antony himself who is being compared to a crocodile), Antony slyly evades the question by giving a vague reply:

> It is shap'd, sir, like itself, and it is as broad as it hath breadth. It is just so high as it is, and moves with it own organs. It lives by that which nourisheth it, and, the elements once out of it, it transmigrates.
> (II, vii, ll. 43-46)

This kind of evasiveness, or double-talk, occurs often in Shakespeare's writing and requires extra patience on the part of the reader.

Shakespeare's Words

As we read Shakespeare's plays, we will encounter uncommon words. Many of these words are not in use today. As *Romeo and Juliet* opens, we notice words like "shrift" (confession) and "holidame" (a holy relic). Words like these should be explained in notes to the text. Shakespeare also employs words which we still use, though with different meaning. For example, in *The Merchant of Venice*, "caskets" refer to small, decorative chests for holding jewels. However, modern readers may think of a large cask instead of the smaller, diminutive casket.

Another trouble modern readers will have with Shakespeare's English is with words that are still in use today, but which mean something different in Elizabethan use. In *The Merchant of Venice*, Shakespeare uses the word "straight" (as in "straight away") where we would say "immediately." Here, the modern reader is unlikely to carry away the wrong message, however, since the modern meaning will simply make no sense. In this case, textual notes will clarify a phrase's meaning. To cite another example, in *Romeo and Juliet*, after Mercutio dies, Romeo states that the "black fate on moe days doth depend" (emphasis added). In this case, "depend" really means "impend."

Shakespeare's Wordplay

All of Shakespeare's works exhibit his mastery of playing with language and with such variety that many people have authored entire books on this subject alone. Shakespeare's most frequently used types of wordplay are common: metaphors, similes, synecdoche and metonymy, personification, allusion, and puns. It is when Shakespeare violates the normal use of these devices, or rhetorical figures, that the language becomes confusing.

A metaphor is a comparison in which an object or idea is replaced by another object or idea with common attributes. For example, in *Macbeth*, a murderer tells Macbeth that Banquo has been murdered, as directed, but that his son, Fleance, escaped, having witnessed his father's murder. Fleance, now a threat to Macbeth, is described as a serpent:

> There the grown serpent lies, the worm that's fled
> Hath nature that in time will venom breed,
> No teeth for the present. (III, iv, ll. 29-31, emphasis added)

Similes, on the other hand, compare objects or ideas while using the words "like" or "as." In *Romeo and Juliet*, Romeo tells Juliet that "Love goes toward love as schoolboys from their books" (II, ii, l. 156). Such similes often give way to more involved comparisons, "extended similes." For example, Juliet tells Romeo:

> 'Tis almost morning, I would have thee gone,
> And yet no farther than a wonton's bird,
> That lets it hop a little from his hand
> Like a poor prisoner in his twisted gyves,
> And with silken thread plucks it back again,
> So loving-jealous of his liberty.
> (II, ii, ll. 176-181, emphasis added)

An epic simile, a device borrowed from heroic poetry, is an extended simile that builds into an even more elaborate comparison. In *Macbeth*, Macbeth describes King Duncan's virtues with an angelic, celestial simile and then drives immediately into another simile that redirects us into a vision of warfare and destruction:

> ...Besides this Duncan
> Hath borne his faculties so meek, hath been
> So clear in his great office, that his virtues
> Will plead like angels, trumpet-tongued, against
> The deep damnation of his taking-off;
> And pity, like a naked new-born babe,
> Striding the blast, or heaven's cherubim, horsed
> Upon the sightless couriers of the air,
> Shall blow the horrid deed in every eye,
> That tears shall drown the wind....
> (I, vii, ll. 16-25, emphasis added)

Shakespeare employs other devices, like synecdoche and metonymy, to achieve "verbal economy," or using one or two words to express more than one thought. Synecdoche is a figure of speech using a part for the whole. An example of synecdoche is using the word boards to imply a stage. Boards are only a small part of the materials that make up a stage, however, the term boards has become a colloquial synonym for stage. Metonymy is a figure of speech using the name of one thing for that of another which it is associated. An example of metonymy is using crown to mean the king (as used in the sentence "These lands belong to the crown"). Since a crown is associated with or an attribute of the king, the word crown has become a metonymy for the king. It is important to understand that every metonymy is a synecdoche, but not every synecdoche is a metonymy. This rule is true because a metonymy must not only be a part of the root word, making a synecdoche, but also be a unique attribute of or associated with the root word.

Synecdoche and metonymy in Shakespeare's works is often very confusing to a new student because he creates uses for words that they usually do not perform. This technique is often complicated and yet very subtle, which makes it difficult for a new student to dissect and understand. An example of these devices in one of Shakespeare's plays can be found in *The Merchant of Venice*. In warning his daughter, Jessica, to ignore the Christian revelries in the streets below, Shylock says:

> Lock up my doors; and when you hear the drum
> And the vile squealing of the wry-necked fife,
> Clamber not you up to the casements then...
> (I, v, ll. 30-32)

The phrase of importance in this quote is "the wry-necked fife." When a reader examines this phrase it does not seem to make sense; a fife is a cylinder-shaped instrument, there is no part of it that can be called a neck. The phrase then must be taken to refer to the fife-player, who has to twist his or her neck to play the fife. Fife, therefore, is a synecdoche for fife-player, much as boards is for stage. The trouble with understanding this phrase is that "vile squealing" logically refers to the sound of the fife, not the fife-player, and the reader might be led to take fife as the instrument because of the parallel reference to "drum" in the previous line. The best solution to this quandary is that Shakespeare uses the word fife to refer to both the instrument and the player. Both the player and the instrument are needed to complete the wordplay in this phrase, which, though difficult to understand to new readers, cannot be seen as a flaw since Shakespeare manages to convey two meanings with one word. This remarkable example of synecdoche illuminates Shakespeare's mastery of "verbal economy."

Shakespeare also uses vivid and imagistic wordplay through personification, in which human capacities and behaviors are attributed to inanimate objects. Bassanio, in *The Merchant of Venice*, almost speechless when Portia promises to marry him and share all her worldly wealth, states "my blood speaks to you in my veins..." (III, ii, l. 176). How deeply he must feel since even his blood can speak. Similarly, Portia, learning of the penalty that Antonio must pay for defaulting on his debt, tells Salerio, "There are some shrewd contents in yond same paper/That steals the color from Bassanio's cheek" (III, ii, ll. 243-244).

Another important facet of Shakespeare's rhetorical repertoire is his use of allusion. An allusion is a reference to another author or to an historical figure or event. Very often Shakespeare alludes to the heroes and heroines of Ovid's *Metamorphoses*. For example, in Cymbeline an entire room is decorated with images illustrating the stories from this classical work, and the heroine, Imogen, has been reading from this text. Similarly, in *Titus Andronicus*, characters not only read directly from the *Metamorphoses*, but a subplot re-enacts one of the *Metamorphoses'* most famous stories, the rape and mutilation of Philomel.

Another way Shakespeare uses allusion is to drop names of mythological, historical, and literary figures. In *The Taming of the Shrew*, for instance, Petruchio compares Katharina, the woman whom he is courting, to Diana (II, i, l. 55), the virgin goddess, in order to suggest that Katharina is a man-hater. At times, Shakespeare will allude to well-known figures without so much as mentioning their names. In *Twelfth Night*, for example, though the Duke and Valentine are ostensibly interested in Olivia, a rich countess, Shakespeare asks his audience to compare the Duke's emotional turmoil to the plight of Acteon, whom the goddess Diana transforms into a deer to be hunted and killed by Acteon's own dogs:

Duke: That instant was I turn'd into a hart,
           And my desires, like fell and cruel hounds,
           E'er since pursue me.
           [...]
Valentine: But like a cloistress she will veiled walk,
           And water once a day her chamber round....
           (I, i, l. 20 ff.)

Shakespeare's use of puns spotlights his exceptional wit. His comedies in particular are loaded with puns, usually of a sexual nature. Puns work through the ambiguity that results when multiple senses of a word are evoked; homophones often cause this sort of ambiguity. In *Antony and Cleopatra*, Enobarbus believes "there is mettle in death" (I, ii, l. 146), meaning that there is "courage" in death; at the same time, mettle suggests the homophone metal, referring to swords made of metal causing death. In early editions of Shakespeare's work there was no distinction made between the two words. Antony puns on the word "earing," (I, ii, ll. 112-114) meaning both plowing (as in rooting out weeds) and hearing: he angrily sends away a messenger, not wishing to hear the message from his wife, Fulvia: "...O then we bring forth weeds,/

when our quick minds lie still, and our ills told us/Is as our earing."
If ill-natured news is planted in one's "hearing," it will render an
"earing" (harvest) of ill-natured thoughts. A particularly clever pun,
also in A*ntony and Cleopatra,* stands out after Antony's troops have
fought Octavius's men in Egypt: "We have beat him to his camp.
Run one before,/And let the queen know of our gests" (IV, viii, ll. 1-
2). Here "gests" means deeds (in this case, deeds of battle); it is also
a pun on "guests," as though Octavius' slain soldiers were to be
guests when buried in Egypt.

One should note that Elizabethan pronunciation was in several cases different from our own. Thus, modern readers, especially
Americans, will miss out on the many puns based on homophones.
The textual notes will point out many of these "lost" puns, however.

Shakespeare's sexual innuendoes can be either clever or tedious depending upon the speaker and situation. The modern
reader should recall that sexuality in Shakespeare's time was far
more complex than in ours and that characters may refer to such
things as masturbation and homosexual activity. Textual notes in
some editions will point out these puns but rarely explain them.
An example of a sexual pun or innuendo can be found in *The Merchant of Venice* when Portia and Nerissa are discussing Portia's past
suitors using innuendo to tell of their sexual prowess:

> Portia: I pray thee, overname them, and as thou
>   namest them, I will describe them, and
>   according to my description level at my
>   affection.
> Nerissa: First, there is the Neapolitan prince.
> Portia: Ay, that's a colt indeed, for he doth nothing but
>   talk of his horse, and he makes it a great
>   appropriation to his own good parts that he can
>   shoe him himself. I am much afeard my lady his
>   mother played false with the smith.
>   (I, ii, ll. 35-45)

The "Neapolitan prince" is given a grade of an inexperienced
youth when Portia describes him as a "colt." The prince is thought

to be inexperienced because he did nothing but "talk of his horse" (a pun for his penis) and his other great attributes. Portia goes on to say that the prince boasted that he could "shoe him [his horse] himself," a possible pun meaning that the prince was very proud that he could masturbate. Finally, Portia makes an attack upon the prince's mother, saying that "my lady his mother played false with the smith," a pun to say his mother must have committed adultery with a blacksmith to give birth to such a vulgar man having an obsession with "shoeing his horse."

It is worth mentioning that Shakespeare gives the reader hints when his characters might be using puns and innuendoes. In *The Merchant of Venice*, Portia's lines are given in prose when she is joking, or engaged in bawdy conversations. Later on the reader will notice that Portia's lines are rhymed in poetry, such as when she is talking in court or to Bassanio. This is Shakespeare's way of letting the reader know when Portia is jesting and when she is serious.

Shakespeare's Dramatic Verse

Finally, the reader will notice that some lines are actually rhymed verse while others are in verse without rhyme; and much of Shakespeare's drama is in prose. Shakespeare usually has his lovers speak in the language of love poetry which uses rhymed couplets. The archetypal example of this comes, of course, from *Romeo and Juliet*:

> The grey-ey'd morn smiles on the frowning night,
> Check'ring the eastern clouds with streaks of light,
> And fleckled darkness like a drunkard reels
> From forth day's path and Titan's fiery wheels.
> (II, iii, ll. 1-4)

Here it is ironic that Friar Lawrence should speak these lines since he is not the one in love. He, therefore, appears buffoonish and out of touch with reality. Shakespeare often has his characters speak in rhymed verse to let the reader know that the character is acting in jest, and vice-versa.

Perhaps the majority of Shakespeare's lines are in blank verse, a form of poetry which does not use rhyme (hence the name blank) but still employs a rhythm native to the English language, iambic pentameter, where every second syllable in a line of ten syllables receives stress. Consider the following verses from *Hamlet*, and note the accents and the lack of end-rhyme:

> The síngle ánd pecúliar lífe is bóund
> With áll the stréngth and ármor óf the mínd
> (III, iii, ll. 12-13)

The final syllable of these verses receives stress and is said to have a hard, or "strong," ending. A soft ending, also said to be "weak," receives no stress. In *The Tempest*, Shakespeare uses a soft ending to shape a verse that demonstrates through both sound (meter) and sense the capacity of the feminine to propagate:

> and thén I lóv'd thee
> And shów'd thee áll the quálitíes o' th' ísle,
> The frésh spríngs, bríne-pits, bárren pláce and fértile.
> (I, ii, ll. 338-40)

The first and third of these lines here have soft endings.

In general, Shakespeare saves blank verse for his characters of noble birth. Therefore, it is significant when his lofty characters speak in prose. Prose holds a special place in Shakespeare's dialogues; he uses it to represent the speech habits of the common people. Not only do lowly servants and common citizens speak in prose, but important, lower class figures also use this fun, at times ribald, variety of speech. Though Shakespeare crafts some very ornate lines in verse, his prose can be equally daunting, for some of his characters may speechify and break into double-talk in their attempts to show sophistication. A clever instance of this comes when the Third Citizen in *Coriolanus* refers to the people's paradoxical lack of power when they must elect Coriolanus as their new leader once Coriolanus has orated how he has courageously fought for them in battle:

> We have power in ourselves to do it, but it is
> a power that we have no power to do; for if he show us his
> wounds and tell us his deeds, we are to put our tongues into

those wounds and speak for them; so, if he tell us his noble
deeds, we must also tell him our noble acceptance of them.
Ingratitude is monstrous, and for the multitude to be
ingrateful were to make a monster of the multitude, of the
which we, being members, should bring ourselves to be
monstrous members.

(II, ii, ll. 3-13)

Notice that this passage contains as many metaphors, hideous
though they be, as any other passage in Shakespeare's dramatic verse.

When reading Shakespeare, paying attention to characters who
suddenly break into rhymed verse, or who slip into prose after
speaking in blank verse, will heighten your awareness of a
character's mood and personal development. For instance, in
Antony and Cleopatra, the famous military leader Marcus Antony
usually speaks in blank verse, but also speaks in fits of prose (II, iii,
ll. 43-46) once his masculinity and authority have been questioned.
Similarly, in *Timon of Athens*, after the wealthy Lord Timon abandons the city of Athens to live in a cave, he harangues anyone whom
he encounters in prose (IV, iii, l. 331 ff.). In contrast, the reader
should wonder why the bestial Caliban in *The Tempest* speaks in
blank verse rather than in prose.

Implied Stage Action

When we read a Shakespearean play, we are reading a performance text. Actors interact through dialogue, but at the same time
these actors cry, gesticulate, throw tantrums, pick up daggers, and
compulsively wash murderous "blood" from their hands. Some of
the action that takes place on stage is explicitly stated in stage di-
rections. However, some of the stage activity is couched within the
dialogue itself. Attentiveness to these cues is important as one con-
ceives how to visualize the action. When Iago in *Othello* feigns concern for Cassio whom he himself has stabbed, he calls to the
surrounding men, "Come, come:/Lend me a light" (V, i, ll. 86-87). It
is almost sure that one of the actors involved will bring him a torch
or lantern. In the same play, Emilia, Desdemona's maidservant, asks
if she should fetch her lady's nightgown and Desdemona replies,
"No, unpin me here" (IV, iii, l. 37). In *Macbeth*, after killing Duncan,

Macbeth brings the murder weapon back with him. When he tells his wife that he cannot return to the scene and place the daggers to suggest that the king's guards murdered Duncan, she castigates him: "Infirm of purpose/Give me the daggers. The sleeping and the dead are but as pictures" (II, ii, ll. 50-52). As she exits, it is easy to visualize Lady Macbeth grabbing the daggers from her husband.

For 400 years, readers have found it greatly satisfying to work with all aspects of Shakespeare's language—the implied stage action, word choice, sentence structure, and wordplay—until all aspects come to life. Just as seeing a fine performance of a Shakespearean play is exciting, staging the play in one's own mind's eye, and revisiting lines to enrich the sense of the action, will enhance one's appreciation of Shakespeare's extraordinary literary and dramatic achievements.

Historical Background

As You Like It was probably written in 1599 or 1600, at the midway point of Shakespeare's career as a playwright. His principal source for the play was Thomas Lodge's pastoral romance, *Rosalynde*. Lodge's novel, published in 1590, was in turn adapted from *The Tale of Gamelyn*, a 14th-century narrative poem. Shakespeare rewrote the story even further; he introduced new themes and created a number of new characters including Jaques, Touchstone, William, and Audrey. He also gave his characters far more depth and dimension than they had in Lodge's novel and added humor to the storyline.

Pastoral romance—a romantic story that takes place in a rural of forest setting—was a popular category of literature and drama in Shakespeare's time. Love stories of innocent shepherds and shepherdesses and tales of woodland adventure were then in vogue. Shakespeare, a practical man of the theatre, created a play that he knew would appeal to his audience. The wrestling scene and the clowning of the rustic shepherds would have captured the attention of the groundlings, while the sophisticated wordplay would have impressed educated playgoers in the galleries. George Bernard Shaw felt that Shakespeare, in calling the play *As You Like It*, was commenting disparagingly on standards of contemporary theatrical taste. Yet it seems unlikely that Shakespeare had purely commercial considerations in mind when he wrote this play, for *As You Like It* does not adhere strictly to the conventions of pastoral romance. It satirizes them as well. The Forest of Arden is in many ways an idealized, fairy tale setting for the play, but it is also a place where "winter and rough weather" present hardships and wild beasts lurk as a threat. Shaw may have been correct, however, in his observation that Shakespeare was losing interest in crowd-pleasing comedies. Soon after he wrote *As You Like It*, Shakespeare abandoned comedy and turned to the composition of his major tragedies.

According to theatrical legend, Shakespeare—an actor as well as a playwright—played the old servant, Adam, when the play was presented by the Lord Chamberlain's Men (later the King's Men), the acting company of which he was a member. We have evidence that suggests this play was performed before King James I in 1603. In all likelihood it remained in the repertory of Shakespeare's company for a number of years after it was written.

As You Like It, although neglected in performance for more than a century after Shakespeare's death in 1616, has been a popular play on the stage ever since. It was revived in England for the first time in 1723 in an adaptation called *Love In A Forest*. This version of the play interpolated passages from other Shakespearean dramas and comedies, notably *A Midsummer Night's Dream*. Shakespeare's original was restored to the theatre seventeen years later. In the 19th century *As you Like It* was staged by a number of eminent English actor-managers including Charles Kean and William Charles Macready. In late nineteenth century America, especially, the play became a favorite with audiences. Rosalind found noteworthy interpreters in Helena Modjeska, Mary Anderson, Ada Rehan, and Julia Marlowe.

More recently, the role of Rosalind has attracted a number of leading actresses including Peggy Ashcroft, Katharine Hepburn, and Vanessa Redgrave. In 1967, the National Theatre of Great Britain staged an all-male production of the play, and in 1991 England's experimental Cheek By Jowl company mounted a similar production. Thus, modern audiences were introduced to a theatrical convention of Shakespeare's time, when young men played all the women's roles. Both productions were well received by audiences and critics and subsequently toured the United States. Also note-worthy is the Renaissance Theatre Company's 1988 Edwardian dress production in London with Kenneth Branagh as Touchstone. Today, when there are more than three hundred Shakespeare festivals worldwide, *As You Like It* remains one of the Bard's most well-loved and frequently produced comedies.

Master List of Characters

Duke Senior—*An exiled Duke, living in banishment in the Forest of Arden.*

Duke Frederick—*Duke Senior's brother; usurper of his dukedom.*

Amiens—*A courtier and singer who attends Duke Senior in exile.*

First and Second Lords—*Courtiers who attend Duke Senior in exile.*

Jaques—*A melancholy philosopher who resides with the exiled Duke Senior in the Forest of Arden.*

Le Beau—*A foppish courtier attending Duke Frederick.*

Charles—*A wrestler at the court of Duke Frederick.*

Oliver—*Eldest son of the late Sir Rowland de Boys and heir to his father's estate.*

Jaques de Boys—*The middle son of the late Sir Rowland de Boys.*

Orlando—*Youngest son of the late Sir Rowland de Boys who falls in love with Rosalind.*

Adam—*A loyal, elderly servant in the household of the late Sir Rowland de Boys who accompanies Orlando to the Forest of Arden.*

Dennis—*Another servant in the household of the late Sir Rowland de Boys.*

Touchstone—*A clown at the court of Duke Frederick who accompanies Rosalind and Celia into exile.*

Sir Oliver Martext—*A clergyman.*

Corin—*An old shepherd who lives near the Forest of Arden.*

Silvius—*A young, lovelorn shepherd.*

William—*A simpleminded young man.*

Hymen—*The god of marriage.*

Rosalind—*Daughter of the banished Duke Senior who falls in love with Orlando.*

Celia—*Rosalind's loyal friend and daughter of Duke Frederick.*

Phebe—*A shepherdess.*

Audrey—*A country wench.*

Summary of the Play

Orlando, youngest son of the late Sir Rowland de Boys, complains to Adam, an elderly family servant, that his brother Oliver has unfairly withheld his late father's inheritance and prevented him from being educated as a gentleman. Oliver enters and a heated argument ensues. When Oliver learns that his brother plans to challenge Charles, Duke Frederick's hulking wrestler, he plots with Charles to break his brother's neck during the match.

The next day Duke Frederick, his daughter Celia, and his niece Rosalind witness the competition. Charles has subdued his first three opponents, but Orlando manages to defeat his adversary. Duke Frederick is infuriated when he learns the identity of Orlando's father, in life his bitter enemy, but Rosalind is captivated by Orlando and gives him a chain from her neck as a reward for his victory. Orlando is immediately taken by her charm, yet he finds himself speechless to thank her.

Rosalind, daughter of the banished Duke Senior whom Frederick has usurped, tells Celia that she has fallen in love with Orlando. Duke Frederick has allowed Rosalind to remain at court because of her friendship with his daughter, but now he banishes her, despite Celia's pleas to allow her to remain. Rosalind and Celia make plans to join Rosalind's father in the Forest of Arden. They decide to travel in disguise, Rosalind as Ganymede, a young man, and Celia as Aliena, a peasant girl. Touchstone, Duke Frederick's court jester, agrees to accompany them.

Duke Frederick is enraged when he learns that his daughter and Rosalind have fled. He believes Orlando is with them and plans a search party, led by Oliver, to find them. Orlando, meanwhile, has learned from Adam that Oliver is plotting to have him killed and they make plans to leave the court for the countryside.

Rosalind and Celia, now in disguise, arrive in the Forest of Arden along with Touchstone. There they overhear a young shepherd, Silvius, tell an old Shepherd, Corin, of his love for Phebe, a shepherdess who has spurned his affections. Orlando and Adam, in the meantime, have arrived in another part of the forest. Adam becomes weak with hunger and Orlando sets out in search of food. He soon discovers the banished Duke Senior and his court and confronts them with his sword drawn. Duke Senior greets him with kindness, however, and invites him to share in his feast. Orlando agrees and leaves to bring Adam to safety.

Obsessed by his love for Rosalind, Orlando writes poems about her and hangs them on trees. Rosalind discovers the poems and is critical of their literary merit, but when she learns they are by Orlando, she has a change of heart. She meets Orlando, who does not recognize her in her male disguise, and offers to cure him of his lovesickness if he will court her as if she were Rosalind. Touchstone, in the meantime, has begun courting Audrey, a goatherd, and Silvius has continued to pursue the shepherdess he loves. Phebe, however, has fallen in love with Rosalind in her Ganymede disguise.

Orlando meets with Rosalind and tells her how he would charm and win his beloved. Oliver arrives in the forest soon afterward and tells Rosalind and Celia that Orlando, unaware of Oliver's identity, had rescued him from a lioness while he slept beneath a tree. He tells them he is Orlando's brother, and that he and Orlando have reconciled. When he reveals that Orlando was wounded by the lioness, Rosalind faints.

Oliver confesses to Orlando that he has fallen in love with Celia. Orlando tells Rosalind that his brother's marriage is to take place the next day and wishes he could marry his own beloved. Rosalind, still in disguise, tells him that through "magic" she will make her appear. She also pledges to help Silvius and Phebe. Touchstone tells Audrey that they, too, will be married on the morrow.

The next day, Rosalind reveals her true identity and she and Orlando, Oliver and Celia, and Silvius and Phebe are married before the banished Duke. Jaques de Boys, the middle son of Sir

Rowland, brings the news that Duke Frederick has met an old religious hermit and has decided to forsake the world and restore his brother's dukedom. The newly united couples dance and Rosalind speaks the epilogue.

Estimated Reading Time

This play should take the average student about five hours to read. It will be helpful to divide your reading time into five one-hour sittings for each of the play's five acts. Shakespeare's language can be difficult for students who are unfamiliar with it, so each act should be read carefully on a scene by scene basis to ensure understanding.

SECTION TWO

Act I

Act I, Scene 1

New Characters:

Orlando: *youngest son of the late Sir Rowland de Boys*

Adam: *an elderly servant in the household of the late Rowland de Boys*

Dennis: *another servant in the household*

Oliver: *eldest son of the late Sir Rowland de Boys and inheritor of his father's estate*

Charles: *Duke Frederick's wrestler*

Summary

Scene 1, set in the orchard of the de Boys family, begins with the entrance of Orlando de Boys and Adam, an elderly servant. Orlando complains to Adam that his late father had bequeathed him a thousand crowns and requested that his oldest brother Oliver provide for his education as a gentleman. Although Oliver has kept the second brother of the family at school, he has treated his youngest brother no better than one of his horses or oxen and has refused to honor his father's will.

Oliver enters and a violent quarrel ensues as Orlando confronts his brother with his resentment. Oliver strikes Orlando, but Orlando puts a wrestler's grip on his brother and subdues him. Adam parts the brothers and Orlando asks for his rightful inheritance. Oliver

dismisses them harshly. After Orlando and Adam leave, Dennis, a servant, enters and tells Oliver that Charles, Duke Frederick's wrestler, has come to speak with him. Charles brings the news that the old Duke Senior has been banished by his younger brother, Duke Frederick, who has usurped his title and lands. The old Duke and his lords have gone into exile in the nearby Forest of Arden where they are living like Robin Hood and his Merry Men. Rosalind, the old Duke's daughter, has been allowed to remain at court as the result of her friendship with Celia, Duke Frederick's daughter.

Charles tells Oliver that he plans to wrestle the next day before Duke Frederick and has learned that Orlando plans to challenge him. He urges Oliver to tell Orlando to withdraw from the match to avoid bodily harm. Oliver assures Charles that his brother is "a secret and villainous contriver" against his "natural brother" and tells him "I had as lief thou didst break his neck as his finger" during the match. He warns Charles that Orlando might resort to treachery to defeat him. After Charles exits, Oliver confesses that he hates and envies Orlando and hopes the match will bring "an end" to his brother.

Analysis

In Medieval and Renaissance Europe, a system existed known as primogeniture. The land, money, and goods owned by a family often passed by law or by sanctioned custom into the hands of the family's eldest son, to the exclusion of other family members. Thus, Oliver would not have been legally bound (or bound by the customs of the time) to honor the terms of his father's bequests to Orlando. He had a moral obligation, of course, but chose to ignore it.

By establishing Orlando immediately as a young man who has been wronged, Shakespeare engages our sympathy for this character. Even his brother later confesses that he's "gentle ...full of noble device, of all sorts enchantingly beloved." Oliver, on the other hand, is established as an unjust and treacherous character who has deliberately ignored his late father's bequest of money and his wish that he provide for Orlando's education as a gentleman. We also learn that he is willing to resort to dishonest means to see his brother out of the way.

The relationship between Oliver and Orlando is paralleled by the relationship between Duke Frederick and the deposed Duke Senior. In both instances, a brother has been treated unfairly. There is one noteworthy difference, however. Duke Senior is the elder brother and rightful heir to the dukedom. Duke Frederick's usurpation is both immoral and unlawful.

When we learn that Duke Senior and his court-in-exile "fleet the time carelessly as they did in the golden world" we are introduced to one of the play's many themes: the issue of city life versus country life. The court—and the de Boys household—are characterized by animosity and malice, whereas Duke Senior's pastoral existence is the Forest of Arden is idealized.

Act I, Scenes 2 and 3

New Characters:

Rosalind: *daughter of the exiled Duke Senior*

Celia: *daughter of Duke Frederick and Rosalind's loyal friend*

Touchstone: *Duke Frederick's court jester*

Le Beau: *a foppish courtier*

Duke Frederick: *usurper of his brother's dukedom; Celia's father and Rosalind's uncle*

Summary

The next day, Rosalind, daughter of the banished Duke Senior, and Celia, Duke Frederick's daughter, are encountered at Duke Frederick's palace. Celia urges her cousin to "be merry," but Rosalind is still upset by her father's banishment. Celia attempts to cheer her up by pledging her friendship and affection. Rosalind agrees to be joyful for her sake, and to "devise sports." She asks Celia what she would think of falling in love, to which Celia replies that love is best treated as a "sport" rather than in earnest. The young women banter lightheartedly about the caprices of "fortune" and "nature." Touchstone, Duke Frederick's court jester, arrives on the scene. He engages in witty chatter and tells Celia that her

father has summoned her. Le Beau, one of Duke Frederick's courtiers, enters and informs Rosalind and Celia that the wrestling matches are underway. Charles has defeated his first three challengers, doing bodily harm in the process.

Duke Frederick and his court, along with Orlando and Charles, arrive for the next match. Duke Frederick is worried for Orlando's safety and urges his daughter and niece to dissuade him from competing. Their attempts are met by Orlando's firm declaration that "If killed...I shall do my friends no wrong for I have none to lament me; the world no injury, for in it I have nothing." The match begins and Rosalind and Celia cheer for Orlando. Then, to the astonishment to the onlookers, Orlando throws his opponent. Duke Frederick orders the match to a halt. Orlando wants to continue, but Charles is vanquished and is carried off.

Duke Frederick inquires of the victor's name, but when he learns that Orlando is the son of the late Sir Rowland de Boys, an ally of the banished Duke, his manner becomes harsh. "I would thou hadst been son to some man else," he remarks. Although the world esteemed Sir Rowland as honorable, Frederick considered him an enemy. He exits with his court. Rosalind and Celia remain.

Orlando proclaims that he is proud to have been Sir Rowland's son and Rosalind comments that her father "lov'd Sir Rowland as his soul." She gives Orlando a chain from around her neck, but Orlando, who has fallen in love at first sight, is speechless and unable to thank her. Rosalind and Celia exit and Le Beau warns Orlando that the Duke is furious at his victory. He advises him to "leave this place" and also tells him that the Duke has recently "ta'en displeasure 'gainst his gentle niece" since the people "praise her for her virtues" and "pity her for her father's sake." Le Beau exits and Orlando, alone, notes that he must now go from facing "a tyrant Duke" to facing a "tyrant brother." Yet at the same time he has something to cheer his spirits: "heavenly Rosalind."

In Scene 3, also set at Duke Frederick's palace, Rosalind confesses to Celia that she has fallen in love with Orlando. Their conversation grinds to a halt, however, when Duke Frederick enters "with his eyes full of anger" and banishes Rosalind from the court. When Rosalind asks for an explanation she is told, "Thou art thy father's daughter, there's enough." Celia pleads with her father for

Rosalind to remain, but the Duke refuses. Celia tells him that if Rosalind is banished she will go as well. Duke Frederick calls her a fool and exits.

Celia suggests that they join Rosalind's father in the Forest of Arden. Rosalind protests that the journey will be dangerous for young women: "Beauty provoketh thieves sooner than gold." Celia proposes that they travel in disguise and resolves to dress in peasant attire and call herself Aliena. Rosalind, the taller of the pair, decides to dress as a young man and call herself Ganymede. They make plans to lure Touchstone along for the journey to divert them. They exit to pack their "jewels" and "wealth" and view their flight from the court as a journey "to liberty, and not to banishment."

Analysis

The loyal friendship between Rosalind and Celia contrasts sharply with the antagonistic relationship between their fathers and that of Orlando and Oliver. Earlier, we have been told that they were "ever from their cradles bred together" and that "never two ladies loved as they do." Now we see their relationship firsthand. This continues a pattern of hearing about a relationship before it is shown on stage. In the first scene, for example, we heard of Oliver's unjust treatment of Orlando, then Oliver entered and confirmed his account. We already know that Duke Senior and his court are living in the forest of Arden like Robin Hood and his Merry Men; later we will see them doing just that.

Early in the second scene, Shakespeare introduces two additional themes: fortune and nature. Rosalind and Celia engage in witty wordplay in their discussion of these elements. Celia comments that fortune's gifts are not bestowed equally and Rosalind adds that the "goddess" fortune is, by tradition, blind. As we have seen, even those who are gifted by nature can suffer the caprices of fortune. Orlando, for example, is noble by nature, yet fortune has deprived him of his father's bequests. These thematic motifs will recur many times in the play. Later in this scene, for example, Rosalind, after giving Orlando her chain, describes herself as "one out of suits with fortune." This scene also introduces the theme of love, which will be explored in many of its aspects. In the opening exchange between Celia and Rosalind, the platonic love among

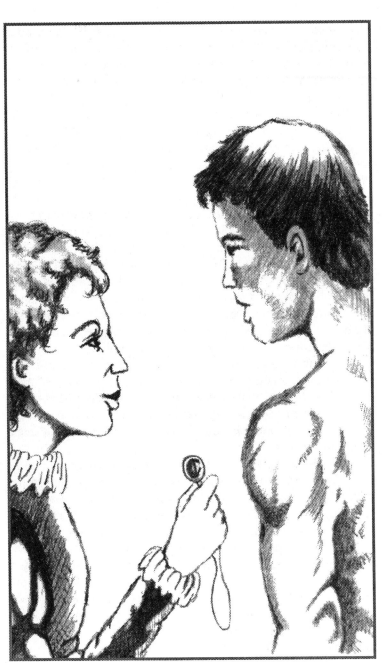

cousins is contrasted with romantic love. Celia advises Rosalind to view romance as a "sport" but not in earnest. By the end of the scene, however, Rosalind will have fallen in love with Orlando. We also learn that Rosalind's father had loved Orlando's father "with all his soul."

The characters of Touchstone and Le Beau serve particular functions in *As You Like It*. Touchstone, a witty court fool, impudent, wise, shrewd, and verbally dextrous, has a special license to speak his mind freely. He comments on the action with subtle irony. When Rosalind and Celia are summoned to the wrestling match after Charles has injured three opponents, for instance, he remarks wryly that "It is the first time that ever I heard breaking of ribs was sport for ladies." In Shakespeare's time, a "touchstone" was the stone on which precious metals were rubbed to test their genuineness. The character of Touchstone similarly exposes the inner natures of those he meets. Le Beau, on the other hand, is revealed through his pompous speech and dandified dress as a character who is affected rather than "natural." He represents the formality of the court as opposed to the freer, more spontaneous life many of the characters will encounter in the Forest of Arden.

In Scene 3, we learn that Rosalind's thoughts have now turned, in part, from her father to the future and her "child's father." As in the previous scene, Shakespeare uses clever wordplay that builds on a wrestling analogy: Celia urges Rosalind to "wrestle with her affections" and comments on her sudden "fall" into "so strong a liking" for Orlando.

Duke Frederick further reveals his villainous nature when he forces Rosalind into banishment as he had earlier banished her father. Celia demonstrates her loyalty to her cousin by resolving to accompany her. Their decision to travel in disguise has a practical purpose, for as Rosalind comments, it is dangerous for women to venture forth alone in the countryside. Her determination to travel in a man's apparel as Ganymede will help to assure their safety.

In classical mythology, Ganymede, a beautiful Trojan youth who was seized and carried to Mount Olympus by Zeus' eagle, was the cup bearer of the gods. By tradition, he was beloved by Zeus, the king of the gods (also known as Jupiter and Jove). When Rosalind declares, "I'll have no worse a name than Jove's own page," many in Shakespeare's audience would have known that this myth, with its connotations of same sex romantic love, would underscore the comic action of the play. This reference also foreshadows the appearance of a mythological god in the final scene.

Rosalind's new identity will also serve a purely dramatic purpose. Disguise was an essential convention of Elizabethan drama and Shakespeare's plays in particular. This device will later prove to be an important element of the plot. Many of the complications in the acts that follow will result from other characters believing that Rosalind is a young man. Thus, the audience (or the reader) is in on a secret that many characters in the play will not know.

With Celia's declaration in the concluding line that the young women are going "to liberty, and not to banishment," Shakespeare again contrasts city life and pastoral life. The court, as we have seen, is a place of tyranny and corruption, yet the Forest of Arden, although not without its perils, will be revealed mainly as an idyllic green world of harmony and understanding.

Study Questions

1. Why does Orlando resent the way he has been treated by his brother Oliver?

2. How does Charles describe the exiled Duke Senior and his court?

3. Why does Duke Frederick allow the daughter of his banished brother to remain at court?

4. What plot does Oliver hatch against Orlando?

5. Why is Orlando warned not to wrestle with Charles?

6. What gift does Rosalind give to Orlando after he wins his wrestling match?

7. How do we know that Rosalind and Orlando have fallen in love at first sight?

8. What warning does Le Beau bring to Orlando after the match?

9. What are the reasons Duke Frederick gives for banishing Rosalind?

10. Why do Rosalind and Celia disguise themselves when they leave the court?

Answers

1. Orlando resents his treatment at his brother's hands because Oliver has ignored the bequests made by their late father. Sir Rowland de Boys left Orlando a thousand crowns and requested that Oliver provide for his education as a gentleman, but Oliver has kept Orlando "rustically at home" and has treated him no better than one of his horses or oxen.

2. Charles describes the exiled Duke and his court as living like Robin Hood and his Merry Men in the Forest of Arden. There they "fleet the time carelessly as they did in the golden world."

3. Duke Frederick has allowed Rosalind to remain at court because of her friendship with his daughter Celia. Charles tells Oliver that "the Duke's daughter her cousin so loves her, being ever from their cradles bred together, that she would have followed her exile, or have died to stay behind her."

4. Oliver plots to have Charles disable or kill Orlando during the wrestling match scheduled for the next day. He tells Charles "I had as lief thou didst break his neck as his finger" and warns him that Orlando may resort to poison or treachery if Charles does not take care of him first.

5. Celia, at Duke Frederick's bidding, warns Orlando that he has seen "cruel proof" of Charles's strength. Charles has seriously injured his first three opponents and Orlando's safety is at stake.

6. Rosalind gives Orlando a chain from around her neck and bids him to "wear this for me."

7. Rosalind tells Orlando, "Sir, you have wrestled well, and over-thrown/ More than your enemies." After Rosalind exits, Orlando proclaims, "O poor Orlando, thou art overthrown!/ Or Charles, or something weaker master thee."

8. Le Beau tells Orlando to "leave this place" because the Duke is angry and there is no telling what he might do.

9. Duke Frederick accuses Rosalind of being a traitor and says he does not trust her. When asked to explain his reasoning he replies, "Thou art thy father's daughter, there's enough."

10. Rosalind and Celia decide to disguise themselves because it would be dangerous for young women to travel alone in the countryside.

Suggested Essay Topics

1. Discuss the concepts of fortune and nature as they apply to Orlando and Oliver.

2. Compare and contrast the relationship of Oliver and Orlando with that of Rosalind and Celia.

3. Explore the ways that Shakespeare uses witty wordplay based on "sport" and "wrestling" analogies to reveal his characters' views on the subject of love.

4. Compare the impressions we get of court life and country life in the first act.

Act II

Act II, Scene 1

New Characters:

Duke Senior: *an exiled duke, living in banishment in the Forest of Arden; Rosalind's father and Celia's uncle*

Amiens: *a courtier and singer who attends Duke Senior*

First and Second Lords: *courtiers who attend Duke Senior in exile*

Summary

Scene 1 takes place in the Forest Arden. Duke Senior tells his "co-mates and brothers in exile" that he finds life in the forest "more sweet" and "free from peril" than life at "the envious court," despite the inconvenience of cold and winter winds. Amiens, one of the Duke's courtiers, agrees, noting that the Duke has turned the misfortune of his banishment into a happy life in the forest. Duke Senior proposes that he and his courtiers embark on a deer hunt, although he regrets having to kill deer "in their own confines." The First Lord replies that Jaques, another courtier, also feels remorse at having to kill animals for food. That day, Jaques had come upon a deer wounded by a hunter. This sight had moved him to tears and philosophical reflection. He had observed cynically that Duke Senior and his courtiers were usurpers and tyrants themselves for frightening and killing the animals in the forest. Duke Senior asks to be taken to the place where Jaques has remained, "weeping and

commenting" upon the fallen deer, for he enjoys encountering Jaques when he is in one of his melancholy moods.

Analysis

In Scene 1, we learn that Duke Senior, although banished from his dukedom and lands, has made the most of his misfortune. Duke Senior's comments on his existence in the Forest of Arden are yet another paean to the pastoral life. Here, we see a far more relaxed atmosphere than we have seen at court. We are in the presence of a new social order. Duke Senior and his court-in-exile have cast aside what is "painted" and "envious." We are also greeted by images of bountiful nature: in the forest, Duke Senior remarks, one can find "tongues in trees, books in the running brooks,/ Sermons in stones, and good in everything." Yet life in the forest, as we learn in Duke Senior's opening speech, also has its hazards, particularly the "icy fang" of the winter wind. Duke Senior is optimistic by nature, however, and he seems undiscouraged by the hardships he and his court have endured. When he mentions that "Here feel we not the penalty of Adam," he is comparing life in the Forest of Arden to man's idyllic existence in the Garden of Eden.

Our introduction to Jaques (pronounced "jay-kweez") continues the pattern of hearing about many of the principal characters before they appear in the play. We learn that Jaques, like Duke Senior, has qualms about killing deer for food. His reaction to this element of life in the forest is much more extreme than the Duke's. Encountering a deer wounded by a hunter's arrow has provoked one of his philosophical moods. Jaques's ironic observation that Duke Senior and his courtiers have usurped the rightful domain of the animals, just as Duke Frederick has usurped his brother's dukedom, has some validity. His pronouncements are reminders that the forest, like the court, is also home to pain and suffering.

Unlike the court, however, this society is a place where diverse types coexist in harmony. It is permissive haven for a misanthrope such as Jaques. Yet it is apparent that Duke Senior, while enjoying Jaques' company and savoring the entertainment he provides, does not take his philosophy seriously. As he remarks, "I love to cope him in these sullen fits,/ For then he's full of matter."

Act II, Scenes 2 and 3

Summary

In Scene 2, set at Duke Frederick's palace, Duke Frederick reveals his anger when he learns that Rosalind, Celia, and Touchstone are missing. A courtier tells him that Orlando is believed to
be in their company. Duke Frederick orders Orlando to be summoned immediately, or for Oliver to be brought should Orlando
be missing. If Orlando is gone, the Duke will make Oliver find his
brother.

Scene 3 takes place at Oliver's house. Adam, in a state of agita-
tion, warns Orlando that he is in mortal danger if he remains at
home. Oliver has learned of Orlando's victory in the wrestling
match, and he plans to burn Orlando's lodgings that very night
while Orlando is sleeping. If that fails, Oliver will resort to other
treacherous means to kill his brother. Orlando is uncertain as to
where he might go, but Adam tells him that any place is better than
remaining at home. Orlando protests that with no money of his
own, his only options would be to "beg for food" or to make "a thiev-
ish living on the common road." Adam tells Orlando that he has
saved five hundred crowns during his years of service to Orlando's
late father, which he had set aside for his old age. He offers Orlando the money and begs to accompany him wherever he goes.
Orlando, moved by Adam's loyalty, invites him to share his journey
into exile.

Analysis

These brief scenes contrast the villainy of Duke Frederick and
Oliver with the noble natures of Adam and Orlando. Adam is in
many ways a model of virtue. From the age of seventeen "till now
almost fourscore" he has served Sir Rowland de Boys and his household faithfully. He has managed to save five hundred crowns by
leading an exemplary life. In his youth he avoided "hot and rebel-
lious liquors" and other vices. Orlando comments admiringly that
Adam is "not for the fashion of these times"—an allusion to the
corruption of the court. Yet we can see that Orlando, too, is virtuous. The idea of earning his living as a beggar or a thief is so repug-
nant to him that he is willing to risk remaining at home. Here again,

we see the theme of fortune when Adam tells Orlando at the end of Scene 3, "Yet fortune cannot recompense me better/Than to die well and not my master's debtor."

Act II, Scene 4

New Characters

Corin: *an old shepherd who dwells near the Forest of Arden*

Silvius: *a young shepherd who is in love with Phebe, a shepherdess*

Summary

Rosalind and Celia, now disguised as Ganymede, a young man, and Aliena, a peasant girl, arrive in the Forest of Arden along with Touchstone. All three are weary in body and spirit after their long journey. As they rest, Corin, an old shepherd, and Silvius, a young shepherd, enter. Rosalind, Celia, and Touchstone overhear their conversation. Silvius sighs that he is hopelessly in love with Phebe, a disdainful shepherdess who has spurned his affections. Corin offers his advice. He assures Silvius that in his younger years, he, too, had been driven to madness by love. However Silvius refuses to believe that anyone could love as he does. He remarks that if Corin has never "broke from company/Abruptly as my passion now makes me," he has never experienced love. Distraught, and true to his word, he runs off, calling Phebe's name. After he exits, Rosalind is reminded of her longing for Orlando, and Touchstone recalls one of his own youthful romantic adventures.

Celia, famished, asks Touchstone to inquire if Corin can provide them with food. Corin tells the visitors from the court that he is merely the hired shepherd of an uncharitable landowner and cannot grant their request. He adds, however, that the cottage, land, and sheep owned by the man whose herd he tends are for sale. Silvius is the intended buyer, but at present he is so obsessed by his love for Phebe that he "cares little for buying anything." Rosalind tells Corin to purchase the flock and property for her, and she promises to retain Corin as shepherd and raise his wages.

Analysis

Early in this scene, Rosalind proclaims: "Well, this is the Forest of Arden." This announcement would have served a practical
purpose for Shakespeare's audience. The theatre of Shakespeare's
time featured little or no scenery—a single tree may have sufficed
for the entire forest. Thus, Rosalind's comment would have established the locale.

Rosalind and Celia have now adopted their disguises, in which
they will remain until the last scene of the play. Rosalind comments
early in this scene on the disparity between her outward appearance and her inner feelings: "I could find in my heart to disgrace
my man's apparel and to cry like a woman." In Shakespeare's time,
the role of Rosalind was portrayed by a young man. Elizabethan
audiences would have appreciated the irony of a young man playing a young woman disguised as a man.

The young, lovelorn shepherd was one of the conventions of
pastoral romance. Here we see a romantic infatuation similar to
that felt by Rosalind and Orlando, yet Silvius' yearning for Phebe is
more comically extravagant. He talks about sighs "upon a midnight
pillow," and he refuses to believe that anyone could ever have felt
the same passion he does. Even so, Rosalind is moved by his declarations of love. She is reminded of her own romantic misfortune—
the circumstances of her banishment have kept her away from
Orlando. Touchstone responds to Silvius in a different manner
entirely. His fanciful account of his courtship of Jane Smile satirizes Silvius' lamentations about the ridiculous actions his love for
Phebe have caused him to commit. He was once so much in love,
he comments, that he kissed the cows' udders the hands of his
beloved had milked. His tale of giving his love two pea pods with
the instruction, "wear these for my sake," also parodies Rosalind's
gift of a chain to Orlando in the wrestling scene and her request to
"Wear this for me."

When Touchstone remarks, "When I was at home, I was in a
better place," he wryly argues for the superiority of court life to
country life. Again, we are reminded that the life in the forest is
perhaps not the ideal paradise of pastoral romance. (Note, also,
that Corin's master is of "churlish disposition" and is unlikely
"to find the way to heaven" by his deeds.) The long journey to the

Forest of Arden and removal from the comforts of home have disillusioned Touchstone, but he pragmatically resigns himself to his fate: "travellers must be content." He promptly seeks to content himself by asserting his authority over one whom he considers his inferior. When he hails Corin in an officious manner and tells him he is being addressed by his "betters," we see further evidence of a new social order. Touchstone, formerly the royal fool, will now assume the role of a sophisticated courtier when he is in the company of shepherds.

Act II, Scene 5

New Character:

Jacques: *a melancholy philosopher who resides with Duke Senior in the Forest of Arden*

Summary

This scene is set in a clearing in the Forest Arden. Amiens, one of Duke Senior's courtiers, sings a ballad that celebrates the pastoral life. When Amiens concludes his song, Jaques asks for more. Amiens protests that the music will make Jaques melancholy, but Jaques retorts, "I can suck melancholy out of a song as a weasel sucks eggs. More, I prithee, more!" Jaques persists, and finally Amiens agrees to sing another verse. Amiens tells Jaques that Duke Senior has been looking for him, but Jaques replies that he has been deliberately avoiding the Duke. Amiens sings another stanza, and this time his fellow courtiers join in. In the forest, the song concludes, one will find "no enemy/ But winter and rough weather." Jaques promptly invents a verse of his own that satirizes the idealism of Amiens' lyrics: "If it do come to pass/ That any man turn ass,/ Leaving his wealth and ease/ A stubborn will to please...Here shall he see gross fools as he." Jaques tells Amiens that he is leaving "to go to sleep, if I can." Amiens tells him that he will go to seek the Duke, whose banquet has been prepared.

Analysis

The song that begins this scene is the first of five songs in the play. Its lyrics, with their images of nature, idealize the pastoral life. Again, we are greeted by a reference to the hazards of "winter and rough weather." Yet the declaration, that it is the only "enemy" one might find in the forest, is another reminder that we are a long way from the envious court.

In this scene, we meet Jaques for the first time. He is a multi-faceted character. In Shakespeare's time, he was what was known as a "humors" character. It was common belief at the time that a person's temperament was governed by four "humors," or bodily fluids: blood, yellow bile, black bile, and phlegm. An overabundance of black bile produced melancholy—note that this character is referred to at times as "the melancholy Jaques." Yet melancholy is only one of his moods. In the previous scene, we learned that Jaques had become sentimental and philosophical after discovering the wounded deer. Now we see a more cynical side to his nature.

Like Touchstone, Jaques sees the disadvantages of the pastoral life. Earlier, Touchstone has commented, "now am I in Arden, the more fool, I." In this scene, we hear Jaques saying much the same thing. A man is an ass, he comments, to leave his "wealth and ease" to please his stubborn will in the forest. By nature, he is an argumentative malcontent, eager to take the opposing view to whatever sentiments are expressed by those around him. His satirical parody of Amien' song typifies his cynicism and contrasts sharply with the idealism of Duke Senior and his court-in-exile.

Act II, Scenes 6 and 7

Summary

In another part of the forest, we encounter Adam and Orlando. Adam tells Orlando that he is famished, can journey no further, and is ready to die. Orlando comforts him and promises to bring him to shelter; he will then venture forth in search of food.

In Scene 7, Duke Senior, preparing for his banquet, inquires as to Jaques' whereabouts. Jaques enters immediately afterward.

He is in an ebullient mood, having met Touchstone: "A fool, a fool! I met a fool i' the forest." Touchstone, Jaques recounts, had "railed on Lady Fortune in good terms." When Jaques greeted him with "Good morrow, fool," Touchstone replied wittily, "Call me not fool till heaven hath sent me fortune." Touchstone then drew a sundial from his pocket and used it to illustrate his philosophy. At ten o'clock, it is an hour after nine and an hour before eleven; thus, "from hour to hour, we ripe and ripe/ And then from hour to hour, we rot and rot;/ And thereby hangs a tale."

Jaques claims he was so delighted by Touchstone's comments that he laughed an hour by his dial. He expresses the desire that he, too, might be a fool: "I must have liberty...give me leave/ To speak my mind, and I will through and through/ Cleanse the foul body of th' infected world." Duke Senior remarks that Jaques is an odd choice to do such good, since he has been a libertine. Jaques defends himself by responding that his castigation will not be harmful if he does not name anyone in particular; those who have been criticized justly will realize the truth of his words.

Their exchange comes to a sudden halt when Orlando bursts in with his sword drawn. He commands the Duke and his court to "Forebear, and eat no more!" Jaques replies drolly, "Why, I have eat none yet." Orlando tells him he will not eat until "necessity be served." Duke Senior calmly asks if Orlando has been boldened by his distress and chastises him for his rude manners. Orlando admits that he has been discourteous and tells Duke Senior he has been brought up in civilized society, but he is desperate for food. Duke Senior tells him that force is unnecessary; a gentle request will bring the result he desires. Orlando is surprised by his courtesy: "Speak you so gently? Pardon me, I pray you. I thought that all things had been savage here/ And therefore put I on the countenance/ Of stern commandment." He apologizes for his behavior, sheathes his sword, and tells Duke Senior that before he can accept any food he must find Adam and bring him to safety. Duke Senior promises that the banquet will not begin until he returns.

After Orlando leaves, Duke Senior, moved by Orlando's suffering, tells his courtiers that "we are not all alone unhappy:/ This wide and universal theatre/ Presents more pageants than the scene/ Wherein we play in." Jaques immediately seizes upon his

analogy, commenting: "All the world's a stage, / And all the men and women merely players; / They have their exits and their entrances, / And one man in his time plays many parts, / His acts being seven ages." He describes each of these ages in turn: the infant, the "whining schoolboy," the lover, the soldier, the justice, the "lean and slippered pantaloon," and finally, "second childishness and mere oblivion."

Orlando enters, carrying Adam in his arms, and the Duke invites them to sit down and eat. Duke Senior asks Amiens to provide some music and Amiens obliges, singing another paean to the pastoral life. After he has finished, Duke Senior tells Orlando that as the son of his old friend, Sir Rowland de Boys, he is welcome to remain. He invites Orlando to come to his cave, welcomes Adam, and asks to hear the story of Orlando's fortunes.

Analysis

Adam's near-starvation in Scene 6 further emphasizes the perils of the pastoral life. Like Rosalind, Celia, and Touchstone, Orlando and Adam have had a long and difficult journey. Orlando's devotion to the aged servant again reveals his nobility of character; he repays Adam's kindness with genuine concern.

When we first heard of Jaques he was in a state of despair over the wounded deer; when we saw him first he was sardonic and cynical. At the beginning of Scene 7, we are exposed to another facet of his nature: he is elated, having met Touchstone in the forest. Jaques was ecstatic when Touchstone "railed on Lady Fortune," but he failed to realize that Touchstone was simply parodying his argumentative nature. Touchstone's absurd satire serves to counterbalance Jaques' acerbic criticism of the pastoral life and his cynical view of human nature in general.

This scene features a number of references to time, a motif that will recur in many variations throughout the play. Touchstone's sundial seems particularly inappropriate in the forest, where little light would reach through the trees. His comment that "from hour to hour we ripe and ripe, / And then, from hour to hour, we rot and rot" is a comic foreshadowing of Jaques' "Seven Ages of Man" speech at the end of this scene. Jaques' assertion that he laughed for a hour by Touchstone's dial is ironic, for again he did not realize that Touchstone was satirizing his philosophy.

Jaques' claim that he longs to be a fool, and thus have liberty to speak his mind freely is also ironic, for he speaks his mind at every opportunity. His declaration that if he, too, could wear motley he could "cleanse the foul body of th' infected world" arouses Duke Senior's ire. As one who has sinned, the Duke remarks, he seems an incongruous choice to cure the ills of society. Again, Jaques' observations have some validity, for society, as we have seen it at court, is in need of a cure.

When Duke Senior disarms Orlando with courtesy after Orlando has confronted the Duke and his men with his sword drawn, it is again a reminder than we are in the presence of a new social order, one that is far removed from the "envious court." Orlando's claim to have been well bred seemingly contradicts his statement in Act I, Scene 1 that he has been denied the education of a gentleman. But we know that he is the son of a father who was much admired, and that he has been gifted by nature with many of Sir Rowland's virtues. His innate good qualities have enabled him to transcend his lack of formal education.

Duke Senior's comment after Orlando leaves to bring Adam to safety that "we are not all alone unhappy" introduces yet another hint that the pastoral life is perhaps not as ideal as many of the characters would have it seem. In Act II, Scene 1, Duke Senior extolled his life in the forest, a viewpoint that was echoed in Amiens' first song. Yet here, perhaps because the Duke was reminded of "better days" at court and his own personal misfortune by Orlando's tale of suffering, he admits candidly that there is something "woeful" in his life in exile.

Jaques' "Seven Ages of Man" speech is one of the most famed speeches in all of Shakespeare; it contains some of the Bard's greatest poetry. In this speech, Jaques provides seven impressions of man at varying stages of his life, a further exploration of the theme of time. Yet the canvas he illustrates is selective. For example, we see the infant "mewling and puking" rather than burbling with delight; the schoolboy is "creeping like snail/unwilling to school" rather than making the journey with enthusiasm. Jaques' comments on the lover are in tune with what we have seen of Silvius (and what we will see of Orlando in the scene that follows), but his next two "ages" are limited, for not all men will be soldiers and justices. This speech, in general, reflects the cynical attitude of its speaker rather than offering a well rounded portrait of humanity. Finally, Jaques arrives at old age and the inevitable end: infirmity and death. His tone is rueful and he paints a grim portrait of man "sans teeth, sans eyes, sans taste, sans everything."

By way of contrast, Adam enters immediately afterward. He is almost eighty and weakened by hunger, necessitating that Orlando carry him in his arms. Yet as we know, he is not approaching senility, or "second childishness," as Jaques puts it. He is still vital in spirit, a sharp contrast to Jaques' bleak view of life's fading years.

Jaques' observation that "one man in his time plays many parts" is appropriate, however, for it underscores another major theme of the play: role playing. Rosalind, for example, has been the royal princess and the faithful friend; she has recently assumed the masculine role of Ganymede. Touchstone, as we have seen, played the subservient role of the fool while at court, yet once he is in the Forest of Arden he asserts his superiority to the rustic shepherds, playing the urbane courtier at every opportunity.

Amiens' ballad, "Blow, blow, thou winter wind" is a companion piece to his earlier song. Again, we see a wintery motif juxtaposed with images of a rich, springlike world. This song also echoes the Duke's declaration in Act II, Scene 1 that "Here feel we not.. the icy fang/ and churlish chiding of the winter's wind." Exposure to the elements, while harsh, is preferable to "man's ingratitude" and "friends rememb'red not." Yet here, a wistful not of skepticism creeps in as well: "Most friendship is feigning, most loving mere folly."

This skepticism is immediately refuted by Duke Senior in his welcome to Orlando, for he proclaims: "I am the Duke/That loved your father." And as we will see, love, although making many of the characters appear foolish at times, can also have its lasting rewards.

Study Questions

1. Which two characters express sorrow about the killing of deer in the Forest of Arden?

2. Who is the source of the rumor that Orlando may be in the company of Rosalind, Celia, and Touchstone?

3. Why does Adam urge Orlando to avoid his brother's house?

4. Why does Orlando initially refuse to leave?

5. Which three items of property does Rosalind agree to purchase from Corin's employer?

6. What reason does Jaques give for avoiding Duke Senior?

7. Why does Orlando leave Adam in the forest?

8. Which character from the court does Jaques tell Duke Senior he met in the forest?

9. What reasons does Orlando give for confronting Duke Senior and his courtiers with his sword drawn?

10. How does Duke Senior know that Orlando is the son of his former friend and ally, the late Sir Rowland de Boys?

Answers

1. Duke Senior remarks that "it irks me that the poor dappled fools...Should in their own confines...have their round haunches gored." We also learn that "the melancholy Jaques grieves at that."

2. Hisperia, Celia's waiting gentlewoman, reported that she believed Orlando had accompanied Rosalind, Celia, and Touchstone when they left the court.

3. Adam urges Orlando to leave Oliver's house because Oliver plans to burn Orlando's lodgings while he is asleep. He also tells Orlando that if this plan fails, Oliver will resort to other treacherous means to kill his brother.

4. Orlando initially refuses to leave because he believes he will be reduced to begging, or that he will be forced to become a thief.

5. Rosalind agrees to purchase a cottage, a flock of sheep, and the pasture land where the sheep graze.

6. Jaques tells Amiens that he is avoiding Duke Senior because "He is too disreputable for my company."

7. Orlando leaves Adam in the forest because he is too weak with hunger to accompany Orlando while he searches for food.

8. Jaques tells Duke Senior that he met Touchstone in the forest.

9. Orlando remarks that he is famished, and he tells Duke Senior, "I thought that all things had been savage here,/ And therefore put I on the countenance/ Of stern commandment."

10. Duke Senior knows that Orlando is the son of the late Sir Rowland de Boys because Orlando has "whispered faithfully" that he was. Duke Senior has also noticed that Orlando's face bears a strong resemblance to his father's.

Suggested Essay Topics

1. Discuss the ways in which Shakespeare reveals that life in the Forest of Arden, while in many ways an idealized existence, also has its hardships.

2. Explore the many images of the natural world in the second act.

3. Compare and contrast the many sides of Jaques' character revealed in the scenes in which he is referred to or appears.

4. Discuss the concept of loyalty as it applies to Orlando and Adam in the second act, and the ways in which it defines their characters.

Act III

Act III, Scenes 1 and 2

Summary

At the palace, Duke Frederick commands Oliver to find Orlando and bring him in, dead or alive, within a year. If Oliver fails to do so, his property and goods will be forfeited. Oliver tells Duke Frederick, "I never loved my brother in my life." "More villain thou," Duke Frederick replies. He orders his men to forcibly remove Oliver from the palace and commands that a writ of seizure be placed on Oliver's house and lands.

In Scene 2, we return to the Forest of Arden. Orlando, obsessed by his love for Rosalind, writes poems to her and hangs them on trees. After he resolves to carve the name of his beloved on every tree in the forest, he exits.

Corin and Touchstone enter, and Corin asks Touchstone how he likes the shepherd's life. Touchstone replies with a witty series of contradictions. Although he finds some elements of country life appealing, he misses the liveliness of the court and its good manners. Corin tells him bluntly that courtly manners would be out of place in the country. The formal kissing of hands, he comments, would be inappropriate when the hands of shepherds are greasy from handling their sheep. Corin praises the virtues of his simple life as a shepherd, and Touchstone responds with a series of bawdy jests that satirize the shepherd's calling.

Their conversation is interrupted when Rosalind enters in her Ganymede disguise, reading aloud a love poem she has found on

a tree: "From the east to western Ind/ No jewel is like Rosalind." Touchstone, unimpressed by the "false gallop" of the verses, promptly invents a parody of the poem. He concludes with yet another bawdy jest. Celia happens upon the scene, reading aloud another love poem about Rosalind.

Celia sends Touchstone and Corin away, and she and Rosalind discuss the poems. Rosalind is critical of their style and literary merit, and she is at a loss to identify their author. When Celia finally tells her, after teasing her for her dullness, that the author can only be Orlando, Rosalind is incredulous. She is ecstatic to learn that Orlando has arrived in the forest, but she wonders how her masculine disguise might complicate matters. "Alas the day!" she remarks. "What shall I do with my doublet and hose?" She queries Celia for any bit of news about Orlando.

Their discussion is interrupted by the entrance of Orlando and Jaques. Rosalind and Celia stand aside and eavesdrop on their conversation. Jaques has taken a cynical view of Orlando's romantic infatuation and urges him to "mar no more trees" with his poems, telling him: "The worst fault you have is to be in love." Orlando proclaims that "'Tis a fault I will not change for your best virtue." Jaques retorts by telling Orlando, "I was looking for a fool when I found you." Orlando chides him by commenting that if it is a fool he is seeking, he can look in the brook, for there he will see his own reflection. They exchange parting shots, and Jaques exits.

Rosalind, in an aside to Celia, resolves to speak to Orlando "like a saucy lackey and under that habit play the knave with him." She steps forward and addresses the young man, who does not recognize her in her Ganymede disguise. They banter lightheartedly about time and love. Rosalind cautions Orlando that love is a disease that is best cured. She tells him that "There is a man haunts the forest that abuses our young plants with carving 'Rosalind' on their barks, hangs odes on hawthorns, and elegies on brambles...If I could meet that fancy-monger, I would give him some good counsel." Orlando confesses that "I am he that is so love-shaked" and asks for her remedy. Rosalind wittily catalogues the physical symptoms of a man in love, and she remarks that Orlando seems to have none of them. Orlando protests that he is indeed in love, but Rosalind tells him that "love is merely a madness" and proposes

"curing it." She tells him she has, in the past, cured a lovelorn swain of his "mad humor" by impersonating his fickle mistress, "full of tears" one minute, "full of smiles" the next. She promises that she can heal Orlando's lovesickness as well. Orlando declares that he does not want to be cured, but Ganymede tells him a cure is possible if Orlando will call "him" Rosalind and come to "his" cottage every day to court him. Orlando, pleased by the thought of wooing even a surrogate Rosalind, agrees to the plan.

Analysis

Scene 1 brings the two villains of the play together. Oliver, accustomed to issuing commands to Orlando, now must answer to a more powerful tyrant. Ironically, Duke Frederick remarks that Oliver is a villain for failing to love his brother. Frederick is guilty of this same offense. This brief scene also sets the stage for Oliver's arrival in the Forest of Arden.

In Scene 2, we see Orlando behaving just as Jaques commented the lover does in his "Seven Ages of Man" speech: "Sighing like furnace, with a woeful ballad/Made to his mistress's eyebrow." Here, he is the lovestruck poet of Renaissance tradition. His verses leave something to be desired, but their sentiments are evidently sincere.

Later in this scene, Corin, in his exchange with Touchstone, eloquently defends the virtues of the pastoral life: "I earn that I eat, get that I wear, owe no man hate, envy no man's happiness, glad of other men's good, content with my harm; and the greatest of my pride is to see my ewes graze and my lambs suck." Touchstone, playing the role of a dissatisfied exile, argues wittily that the court, with its good manners, is far superior to the countryside. His speech features a host of amusing contradictions, and at the same time it satirizes the pastoral ideal. But Corin, praising the reality of his rural existence rather than the ideal notions of the pastoral life expressed by Duke Senior and others, rebuts him on nearly all of the points he makes. Here, we are greeted once more by the theme of city life versus country life. Note that Corin, unlike Silvius, is not an idealized shepherd, but rather a more realistically drawn figure who is concerned primarily with the practical details of his trade.

Touchstone's parody of Orlando's poem is apt, for the poem Rosalind has read has a syrupy, sentimental quality and a number of awkward rhymes. Touchstone's bawdy jest at the end of his parody echoes his bawdy comments to Corin in their earlier exchange. His references to sexuality and lust, here and elsewhere, satirize the idealized notions of love expressed by many of the other characters.

The Orlando-Jaques dialogue parallels in its contrasts the Corin-Touchstone exchange in this scene. Earlier we had seen a pairing of opposites in the sophisticated wit and the simple shepherd. Here we see the worldly cynic and the romantic innocent engage in a duel of words. Jaques would like nothing better than to sit down with Orlando and "rail against our mistress the world, and all our misery." Yet Orlando, true to his nature, will have none of it. The attitudes toward romance expressed by Orlando and Jaques reflect the timeless conflicts of youth and age. Orlando's refutation of Jaques' skepticism serves as a prologue to the love scene that follows. Later, Rosalind's encounter with Jaques will serve much the same purpose.

When Rosalind and Orlando banter about time, it recalls Jaques' mention of Touchstone's sundial in an earlier scene. Again, reference to time seems ironic, for while court life (which Touchstone can never escape entirely) is strictly regimented, the Forest of Arden is in many ways a timeless place. As Orlando remarks, "there's no clock in the forest." This comment foreshadows his behavior in later scenes. Rosalind, on the other hand, is far more conscious of time's passing, a disparity that will lead to complications in her relationship with the man she loves. She tells Orlando bluntly that if there is no clock in the forest, "Then, there is no true lover in the forest; else sighing every minute, and groaning every hour, would detect the lazy foot of Time as well as a clock." In sum, if Orlando were a true lover, he would be prompt.

This scene features a number of incongruities. It seems unlikely, for example, that Rosalind, intelligent and quick-witted, would not know immediately that the author of the mysterious love poems is Orlando. We are also asked to accept the fact that Orlando does not recognize the woman he claims to love in her Ganymede disguise. Much of the humor here arises from confusion—the inability of a character to perceive what other characters already know. The audience (or the reader) is also in on the "secret." This type of confusion occurs frequently in Shakespeare's comedies.

Indeed, the entire Forest of Arden is filled with incongruities. The play is set in the Ardennes region of France (note the French names of many of the characters), but the forest is home to a palm tree and olive trees; later, we will hear that a lioness roams there as well. Moreover, the countryside is peopled by typically English shepherds, and there is a reference to the English folk hero, Robin Hood. In fact, there is a real-life Forest of Arden in Warwickshire, not far from Stratford-upon-Avon where Shakespeare was born and raised. No attempt is made, however, to depict this location realistically. Arden is a place that is both real and enchanted.

Initially, Rosalind is panic-stricken upon learning that Orlando had arrived in the forest; she wonders what to do with her doublet and hose. For the moment, she feels trapped in the role she has assumed. Earlier, she had asked Celia, "dost thou think, though I am caparison'd like a man, I have a doublet and hose in my disposition?" However, when Orlando appears, she quickly recovers her wits and realizes that her disguise may, in fact, prove an advantage. Later, when Orlando becomes suspicious of her refined accent, she invents a "history" for her character, telling Orlando she was raised by "an old religious uncle" who taught her to speak and warned her about the folly of love. She asks Orlando bluntly, "But are you so much in love as your rhymes speak?" Although he has written poetry, she remarks, Orlando seems to have none of the traditional signs of a man in love: a lean cheek, disarray in his dress, and so on. She then sets in motion a plan to put Orlando's love to the test by attempting to "cure" him of his "malady." She refers to Orlando's declarations of love as a "sickness," and she disparages the ways of women. When she impersonated a woman in the past to cure another lovelorn swain, she remarks, her methods were so effective that her "suitor" withdrew to a monastery.

Orlando is initially reluctant to be cured, yet ultimately he agrees to the plan. By the end of this scene, Rosalind is clearly in control and relishes her situation. Her playful yet serious investigation of Orlando's true feelings for her will continue in scenes to come.

Act III, Scenes 3-5

New Characters:

Audrey: *a country wench*

Sir Oliver Martext: *a clergyman*

Phebe: *a shepherdess who dwells near the Forest of Arden*

Summary

Touchstone, in a merry mood, enters with Audrey, a goatherd who lives near the Forest of Arden. Jaques also arrives on the scene; he stands aside, eavesdropping on their conversation. Touchstone attempts to woo Audrey, asking, "Am I the man yet? Doth my simple feature content you?" His witticisms are lost on the simple country goatherd, who does not understand the meaning of the word "poetical." Touchstone has no illusions about Audrey's morals; he suspects her of being a "foul slut." Audrey protests that she is not "a slut," but she adds, "I thank the gods I am foul." Jaques, in a series of asides, comments cynically on the scene that is unfolding.

Touchstone tells Audrey that he has met with Sir Oliver Martext, a clergyman who lives nearby. Sir Oliver has promised to meet him in the forest to perform a marriage ceremony. Touchstone realizes, however, that after he is married to Audrey she is likely to be unfaithful to him. He wittily resigns himself to this fact.

Sir Oliver Martext arrives and Touchstone asks him to officiate at the wedding, but Sir Oliver comments that the marriage will not be lawful unless someone is there to give the bride away. Jaques immediately steps forward to volunteer his services. He comments that a man of Touchstone's "breeding" should not be "married under a bush like a beggar" and urges him to go to a church, where a "good priest" might marry him. Touchstone, in an aside, remarks that he prefers to be married by Sir Oliver, for the marriage might not be legal, thus leaving him free to abandon his wife and make a

better marriage. He agrees to listen to Jaques' advice, however, and proclaims, "Come, sweet Audrey./ We must be married, or we must live in bawdry." He exits with Jaques and Audrey, singing merrily, while a bewildered Sir Oliver stares after them.

In Scene 4, Rosalind, close to tears, worries that Orlando may have forsaken her because he has not arrived at the scheduled time for their meeting. Celia reminds her that tears are inappropriate to her masculine disguise; she reassures her cousin that Orlando is simply attending Duke Senior. Rosalind tells Celia that she had met the Duke the previous day. Her father had not recognized her in her disguise, and when the Duke inquired of her parentage, Rosalind answered wittily that it was "as good as he."

Corin enters and tells Rosalind and Celia that Silvius, the love-lorn shepherd they had often asked about, is at that moment woo-ing Phebe, the shepherdess he loves. Corin remarks that if they would care to "see a pageant truly played/ Between the pale com-plexion of true love/ And the red glow of scorn and proud disdain" they are welcome to accompany him. Rosalind agrees, comment-ing: "The sight of lovers feedeth those in love./ Bring us to this sight, and you shall say/ I'll prove a busy actor in their play."

Scene 5 takes place in a nearby part of the forest. Silvius begs the disdainful Phebe for even the smallest kindness: "Sweet Phebe, do not scorn me; do not, Phebe!/ Say that you love me not, but say not so/ In bitterness." Rosalind, Celia, and Corin enter and observe their conversation from a distance. Silvius tells Phebe that if she falls in love one day she will sympathize with his anguish. How-ever Phebe tells him bluntly, "till that time/ Come not near me....As till that time I shall not pity thee."

At this point, Rosalind steps forward to interrupt their conver-sation. She angrily chastises Phebe for being "proud and pitiless," and she tells Silvius that he is foolish to pursue Phebe, since Silvius is "a thousand times a properer man/ Than she is a woman." Phebe, Rosalind remarks, should be thankful to have a good man's love, since she is not the charming beauty she thinks herself to be. "Sell when you can," Rosalind admonishes her, "you are not for all markets." She urges Phebe to love Silvius and to "take his offer" of marriage.

By that time, however, Phebe has become hopelessly capti-vated by Rosalind in her Ganymede disguise. Rosalind attempts to discourage her interest by speaking harshly, telling her, "I am falser than vows made in wine" and "I like you not." She urges Silvius to keep at his courtship, and she tells Phebe to "look on him better/ And be not proud." With that, she turns and exits with Celia and Corin.

Phebe instantly confesses that now she understands what it means to love. Transformed by her encounter with Ganymede, she admits that she feels sorry for Silvius. Again, she tells the lovelorn shepherd that she has no romantic interest in him, but since he can talk of love, she will tolerate his company. She contradicts her statement of a moment earlier, however, by claiming petulantly the Ganymede, though attractive in certain ways, does no really interest her. She resolves to write a taunting letter to the "peevish boy" to repay him for his rudeness. Silvius agrees to deliver the letter after it is written.

Analysis

Touchstone's courting of Audrey in Scene 3 represents a different type of love than those we have already seen. He candidly confesses to Jaques his reasons for wanting to marry his earthy goatherd: "as the ox hath his bow, sir, the horse his curb, and the falcon her bells, so man hath his desires." Here, he burlesques the romantic idealism we have seen in Orlando and Silvius. He is not seeking beauty and wit; he merely wishes to fulfill his physical cravings.

Touchstone's obscene jests with Audrey were a convention of Elizabethan comedy, one that Shakespeare's audience would have looked forward to eagerly. When Touchstone engages in a witty yet introspective series of puns comparing a deer's antlers to the "horns" he expects to wear, he is creating a variation on one of the most popular jokes in Shakespeare's time. In Elizabethan England, "horns" were the symbol of a cuckold, a man whose wife was cheating on him. The world "cuckold" is derived from the cuckoo—a bird that lays its eggs in other birds' nests. According to Elizabethan legend, cuckolds grew horns on their foreheads. Touchstone, pragmatic about the future, resigns himself to the fact this will be his inevitable fate is he marries Audrey.

Scene 4 reveals Rosalind's insecurities about Orlando's true feelings for her. She also discloses the extent of her love for Orlando. She is upset with him for not arriving at the scheduled time of their meeting, but Celia, a calm voice of reason, assures her that Orlando is busy attending Duke Senior. Again, we are greeted by the theme of role playing when Corin invites Rosalind and Celia to witness "a pageant truly played" by observing Silvius' courtship of Phebe, and in Rosalind's subsequent declaration that she will "prove a busy actor in their play."

Lovelorn shepherds such as Silvius were a convention of pastoral romance. In Scene 5, Shakespeare satirizes those conventions by depicting Silvius' unrequited passion as comically excessive. There seems to be no end to his misery. Here, we are exposed to yet another aspect of love. Silvius is much like Orlando in his ardor, but instead of writing poems, he sighs pathetically about the "wounds invisible/ That love's keen arrows make." It is easy to see why Phebe might be weary of his relentless pursuit. Yet Phebe, as Rosalind points out, is no prize herself. She is vain, petulant, and hindered by her false pride. Just as Shakespeare satirizes the lovelorn shepherd in Silvius, he satirizes another familiar literary type, the "poetic shepherdess," in Phebe. Note that Audrey, a rustic goatherd, did not understand the meaning of the word "poetical," yet Phebe speaks in verse and quotes from a poem by one of Shakespeare's contemporaries, Christopher Marlowe, when she proclaims, "Who ever loved that loved not at first sight?"

Rosalind's harsh criticism of the shepherdess has the opposite effect of what is intended, for Phebe is immediately captivated by Rosalind in her Ganymede disguise. Nevertheless, she craftily misleads Silvius by disparaging Ganymede and playing down the extent of her interest. Thus, additional comic complications are added to the plot as the third act draws to a close.

Study Questions

1. What penalty will Oliver face if he fails to find Orlando within a year?

2. What does Orlando do with the love poems he has written to Rosalind?

3. Where does Celia tell Rosalind she saw Orlando?

4. Where does Orlando tell Jaques he can find a fool?

5. What names do Jaques and Orlando call each other when they part?

6. What excuse does Rosalind make when Orlando comments that her accent seems "something finer" than one might expect of a native of the forest?

7. Why does Touchstone prefer to be married by Sir Oliver Martext rather than "a good priest?"

8. What did Ganymede tell Duke Senior when the Duke asked about her parentage?

9. How do we know that Phebe has fallen in love with Rosalind in her Ganymede disguise?

10. What message does Phebe plan to deliver to Ganymede and who will deliver it?

Answers

1. Duke Frederick tells Oliver that if he fails to find Orlando within a year, he will forfeit his lands and goods.

2. Orlando hangs the love poems he has written to Rosalind on trees in the Forest of Arden.

3. Celia tells Rosalind that she saw Orlando "under a tree, like a dropped acorn."

4. Orlando tells Jaques to look in the brook if he is seeking a fool, for there he will see his own reflection.

5. Jaques calls Orlando "Signior Love." Orlando calls Jaques "Monsieur Melancholy."

6. Rosalind tells Orlando that "an old religious uncle" of hers, in his youth a city man, had taught her how to speak.

7. Touchstone prefers to be married by Sir Oliver Martext because he believes that the marriage might not be legal, thus leaving him free to eventually abandon his wife.

8. When Duke Senior, not recognizing his daughter in her disguise, inquired of Rosalind's parentage, she told him her parentage was "as good as he."

9. We know that Phebe has fallen in love with Ganymede when she comments after Rosalind's exit, "'Who ever loved that loved not at first sight?'"

10. Phebe plans to write a "taunting letter" to Ganymede for scorning her. She asks Silvius to deliver the letter, and he agrees.

Suggested Essay Topics

1. Compare and contrast the attitudes toward love expressed by Orlando, Touchstone, Jaques, and Silvius in the third act.

2. Compare and contrast the attitudes of Corin and Touchstone toward country life and city life in Act III, Scene 2.

3. Explore the ways that Rosalind's Ganymede disguise affects her behavior in this act.

4. Discuss the ways in which the developments in the third act foreshadow further comic complications.

Act IV

Act IV, Scene 1

Summary

Rosalind and Celia, still in their disguises, enter with Jaques, who expresses a desire to become better acquainted with Ganymede. Rosalind comments that she has heard that Jaques is "a melancholy fellow." Jaques admits this is true; he tells Rosalind that he likes melancholy better than laughter. Rosalind cautions against going to extremes of either melancholy or mirth, and Jaques retorts that "'tis good to be sad and say nothing." In that case, Rosalind replies wittily, it is good to be a post. Jaques remarks that his melancholy was acquired during his travels abroad, but Rosalind is skeptical of his tale. Orlando enters soon afterward. Jaques bids farewell to Ganymede and departs.

Orlando, late for his rendezvous, casually explains to Rosalind that he has come within an hour of the appointed time. Rosalind chides him for being tardy; true lovers, she reminds him, arrive promptly. She tells him, "I had as lief be wooed of a snail," and she adds mischievously that a snail, like many husbands, has "horns." Women, she reminds him, can't be trusted to be faithful. Orlando protests that his Rosalind is virtuous. "And I am your Rosalind," Ganymede proclaims, elated by the compliment. Celia, worried that Orlando might realize the truth of this statement, quickly interjects, "It pleaseth him to call you so: but he hath a Rosalind of a better leer than you." However Orlando is none the wiser, and Ganymede bids Orlando to "Come, woo me." She asks Orlando

what he would say if the "real" Rosalind were there. Orlando replies that he would kiss before he spoke. Rosalind tells him bluntly it would be better to speak first. After bantering merrily with Orlando, Ganymede plays the devil's advocate, telling him, "I will not have you."

Orlando protests that he would die if this were the case, but Rosalind replies skeptically that "men have died from time to time and worms have eaten them, but not for love." Orlando tells her he would not have his Rosalind "of this mind," for her frown might kill him. Ganymede then agrees to play Rosalind in a more receptive mood. "Ask me what you will, I will grant it," she remarks. Orlando asks her to love him. Rosalind, as Ganymede, replies that she will, "Fridays and Saturdays and all," although she jests that she will also have twenty more men like him, since one cannot have "too much of a good thing." She then asks Celia to perform a mock marriage ceremony. Rosalind and Orlando exchange vows with Celia serving as "priest," but when they have finished, Ganymede cautions that women often change after they are married. She warns Orlando that his Rosalind will be jealous, clamorous, and giddy, will "weep for nothing," and will "laugh like a hyena" when he is trying to sleep.

Orlando tells Ganymede that he must leave for two hours to attend Duke Senior at dinner, but he promises to return. Rosalind warns him not to be late again, telling him that another lateness will prove him a "most pathetical break-promise" and a man unworthy of Rosalind's love. With a pledge to return on time, Orlando exits.

After he is gone, Celia chides Rosalind for having "misused our sex" in her role playing with Orlando. She jokingly threatens to pull off her doublet and hose to reveal her masquerade. Rosalind protests that she is more deeply in love than Celia realizes; My affection hath an unknown bottom, like the Bay of Portugal." She tells Celia that she cannot bear to be out of Orlando's sight and plans to "go find a shadow, and sigh till he come." While Rosalind is sighing, Celia will be doing something far more mundane: taking a nap.

Analysis

Rosalind's reaction to Jaques is similar to Orlando's response in an earlier scene. Again, we are greeted by a classic conflict between youth and age. Rosalind would rather have a fool to make her merry than experience to make her sad. Her romanticism, like Orlando's, stands in sharp contrast to Jaques' cynical view of the world.

In this scene, Jaques attempts to define his melancholy as unique, commenting that it is unlike the scholar's melancholy, the musician's, the soldier's, the lawyer's, the lover's, or the lady's. In sum, he briefly catalogues the varieties of melancholy as he had previously categorized the ages of man at greater length. Elizabethan audiences took particular delight in complex flights of rhetoric such as Jaques offers here; earlier, we heard similarly detailed discussions of fortune, nature, and time.

Jaques remarks that his world weariness is a result of his travels abroad. To Rosalind, however, his speech, dress, and general demeanor seem merely an exaggerated pose. Here, Shakespeare was satirizing the Englishmen of his own time who returned from the Continent and expressed dissatisfaction with life at home. Earlier, Touchstone had stated that "Travellers must be content." Jaques, on the other hand, asserts that his travels have made him a malcontent. We already know that Duke Senior likes to contend with Jaques when he is in his melancholy moods, but he does not take him seriously. Rosalind, the Duke's daughter, seems even less impressed by Jaques' gloomy philosophy.

When Orlando enters the scene, he is almost an hour late for his appointment with Ganymede. Apparently he is caught up in the timelessness of the forest, but Rosalind is not. Jaques notices him when he enters, but Rosalind, peeved at his lateness, ignores him. She comments on the departing Jaques for a moment before turning to greet him with mock surprise: "Why, how now, Orlando, where have you been all this while?" One more lateness, she warns him, and he will be banished from her sight.

Clearly, Rosalind is delighted by the opportunity to again "play the saucy lackey" with the man she loves. The character of Rosalind is one of Shakespeare's most vivacious, charismatic heroines. She is witty and wise, with a playful sense of humor, yet she, too, is not immune to the wonders of love. When she proclaims to Orlando, "I am your Rosalind," she is, of course, speaking the truth. Celia is concerned that Orlando might see through Rosalind's disguise, but

Orlando, in keeping with the play's conventions, gives no indication that he suspects Ganymede's true identity.

As Ganymede, Rosalind has the opportunity to present Orlando with not one but two Rosalinds. The first is somewhat of a skeptic. Playfully, she puts Orlando to the test, mocking his romantic assertions that he will die if Rosalind rejects him. (Note that Orlando, in his comments, echoes Silvius' remarks to Phebe in the previous scene that he, too, will die if Phebe does not love him.) Rosalind quickly rebuts his conventional sentiments, citing the supposedly tragic examples from classical literature of Troilus and Cressida and Hero and Leander. She tells him bluntly, "These are all lies." However when Orlando objects to Ganymede's "characterization," Rosalind tries a different approach: playing "Rosalind" in a more pliant mood. She enjoys hearing Orlando's declarations of love, and her own responses to his wooing and genuine, both here and in the mock wedding that follows.

Afterward, however, she cautions Orlando that "Men are like April when they woo, December when they wed. Maids are May when they are maids, but the sky changes when they are wives." Given the many contrasts we have already seen between the green world of spring and the "icy fang" of winter, her analogy seems apt. Yet here again, Rosalind is playing devil's advocate. She is putting Orlando to the test with generalized observations on the foibles of human nature rather than predicting what might occur in her own marriage. Her comments on "horns" and infidelity, for instance, are made playfully rather than in earnest.

There is probably some truth in Ganymede's warning to Orlando about the "irrational" behavior he might expect from his wife, however, given what we have already seen of Rosalind's many moods. Yet Orlando is undaunted, and Rosalind is reluctant to see him depart to attend the Duke. His response to Ganymede has made it obvious that he loves the "real" Rosalind. After he is gone, Rosalind abandons her role playing. She confesses to Celia that she is deeply in love. However Celia wryly punctures Rosalind's romanticism with bawdy jests and skepticism, just as Rosalind has teased Orlando moments earlier.

Note that Celia, although present throughout this scene, plays a diminishing role as the play progresses. Earlier, Celia commented that the cousins "have slept together,/ Rose at an instant, learned, played, eat together,/ And wheresoe'r we went, like Juno's swans,/ Still we went coupled and inseparable." Yet now we see their relationship changing; Celia is almost silent as Rosalind and Orlando engage in their courting. She is watching her friend's affections being shifted to Orlando, and we are aware that the longstanding relations between the two loving cousins will be transformed as they move toward maturity and marriage.

Act IV, Scene 2

Summary

In another part of the forest, Jaques encounters several Lords bearing the carcass of a deer. He asks which of the Lords killed the deer and suggests that they "present him to the Duke, like a Roman conquerer." He inquires if they have a song for the occasion, which they do. "Sing it," Jaques commands. "'Tis no matter how it be in tune, so it make noise enough." The Lords break into a lusty song that features a play on words comparing a deer's antlers and the "horns" of a cuckold.

Analysis

Jaques' response to meeting the Lords and seeing their slaughtered prey is in sharp contrast to his "weeping and commenting" after encountering a wounded deer in the second act. His response suggests that there may be some truth to Rosalind's accusation that his melancholy and cynicism may in part be a pose. However, there is more than a hint of sarcasm in his suggestion that the deer be given to the Duke like tribute paid to a Roman conquerer.

The lyrics to the song, with their references to "horns" and cuckoldry, again evoke a comic motif we have heard in the conversations of Touchstone and Rosalind. Touchstone's comments have been witty yet pragmatic, given that he is planning to marry Audrey, and Rosalind's remarks were designed principally to put Orlando to the test by disparaging women's virtues and romantic love in general. Here, the song seems designed to counterbalance the lyrical romanticism of Rosalind's declarations at the end of the

previous scene. Note that Shakespeare often juxtaposes romantic sentiments with a refutation of the romantic ideal. After Rosalind reads aloud one of Orlando's poems, for example, we are greeted by Touchstone's bawdy parody.

Act IV, Scene 3

Summary

It is now past two o'clock, the appointed hour of Rosalind and Orlando's meeting, but Orlando has not appeared. Celia teases Rosalind by telling her that Orlando is so deeply in love that he has probably fallen asleep.

Silvius enters and presents Ganymede with the letter Phebe has written to her. He confesses that he does not know the contents, but tells her that he believes the letter was written in anger, judging by Phebe's expression while she was writing it. Rosalind pretends to Silvius that Phebe has been harsh in her criticism of Ganymede. She playfully accuses Silvius of writing the letter himself and comments that it appears to be in a man's handwriting. But Silvius innocently denies any knowledge of the letter's contents.

Rosalind reads the letter aloud, insisting all the while that Phebe is insulting Ganymede. However it is actually a love letter, and when Silvius hears Phebe's impassioned sentiments he realizes the truth and is heartbroken. Celia feels sorry for Silvius, but Rosalind comments that he is foolish to love a woman as false of Phebe. She commands Silvius to return to the shepherdess to inform her that Ganymede will love her only when she loves Silvius. She also tells him to deliver the message that Ganymede will "never have her" unless Silvius pleads for her cause. Silvius exits meekly to do her bidding.

As stranger enters immediately afterward, inquiring as to the whereabouts of "that youth" whom Orlando "calls his Rosalind." It is Orlando's brother Oliver, and he is bearing a token from Orlando: a bloody handkerchief. He explains why Orlando was unable to keep his promise to return at two o'clock. While wandering in the forest, Orlando had come across "a wretched, ragged man, o'er grown with hair" sleeping beneath an ancient oak tree. A snake was entwined around his neck, but seeing Orlando, the snake slithered away. Greater peril lay nearby, however, for a hungry lioness was lurking in the bushes. Orlando saw the lioness, yet approached the sleeping man and discovered that it was his brother who had plotted to take his life. Twice, Orlando thought about leaving Oliver in peril, but his kind nature, "nobler ever than revenge," led him to wrestle with the lioness, whom he quickly killed.

Oliver admits to Rosalind and Celia that he is the man Orlando rescued, the same man who had often contrived to kill his younger brother. He tells them that he is no longer the villain he once was; grateful to Orlando for saving his life, he has reconciled with his brother. After Oliver related to Orlando the story of how he had arrived in the forest, Orlando had taken him to meet Duke Senior. While visiting the Duke at his cave, Orlando discovered that the lioness had wounded his arm. Oliver bound his wound, and Orlando had sent his brother into the forest with the bloody handkerchief to find "the shepherd youth/ That he in sport doth call his Rosalind," and to apologize for his missed appointment. When Rosalind hears that Orlando has been wounded and realizes the handkerchief is stained with his blood, she faints.

Oliver, unaware that Ganymede is Rosalind in disguise, observes that "many will swoon when they look on blood," but he chides her for lacking "a man's heart." Rosalind acknowledges that his last statement is true, but she makes the excuse that she was simply absorbed in her role. She asks Oliver to tell his brother "how well I counterfeited." Yet Oliver observes that Ganymede's passion for Orlando seems real. Celia remarks that Ganymede looks pale, and Oliver and Celia lead her away toward her cottage.

Analysis

Orlando, as we have seen, is a young man of many virtues, but promptness is not one of them. In the first scene of the act, he was warned by Rosalind that his next lateness would be his last, thus setting up potential complications if he is late to their next meeting. But this time, as we learn, he has a good excuse.

Rosalind, as Ganymede, toys with Silvius in much the same way as she had teased Orlando in Act IV, Scene 1. She pretends that Phebe's letter is what Silvius had supposed it to be, and she

accuses him of writing it himself. Here again, Phebe is in many ways the "poetic shepherdess" of pastoral romance (her love letter is, of course written in verse), yet Rosalind punctures the convention by making fun of her "leathery" hands. When she realizes how upset Silvius is by the actual contents of the letter, she becomes justifiably irate at his infatuation, calling him a "tame snake." She then institutes a practical plan that may cure Phebe of her false pride and bring the lovers together.

Oliver's conversion seems miraculous. However, such instantaneous changes were a convention of Elizabethan drama, one that Shakespeare's audience would have accepted. The play, as we have seen, contains a number of realistic elements, yet Oliver's transformation is in keeping with the fairy tale nature of much of the story. Even so, his metamorphosis may not have been as sudden as it might seem. Oliver, when last seen in Act III, Scene 1, was banished by a more powerful tyrant than himself, and we learn that he wandered extensively, enduring the hardships of the forest, perhaps giving him reasons to contemplate his actions in the past.

Throughout much of the play, Rosalind demonstrates "masculine" confidence while in her disguise. Yet she loses her courage when she is confronted by the sight of the handkerchief soaked with Orlando's blood. Much of the comedy in the latter part of this scene results from Rosalind behaving in an "unmasculine" manner. The dialogue features a good deal of dramatic irony: Oliver, for example, chides Ganymede for lacking a man's heart, and Ganymede comments, "I should have been a woman by right." Rosalind has "counterfeited" her outward appearance to play the role of Ganymede (and indeed, she claims to Oliver that she has counterfeited a woman so well that she faints at the sight of blood), yet her emotions are genuine.

Oliver, like his brother, is fooled by Rosalind's disguise, although by the end of this scene it is apparent that the disguise is wearing thin. (Note that Celia slips in calling Rosalind "Cousin Ganymede.") Orlando has now been put to the test and has passed; again, we feel the depth of Rosalind's love for him. The masquerade is rapidly losing its attraction, and the events of the play are winding to a close.

Study Questions

1. What is Rosalind's response when Orlando fears "her frown might kill" him?

2. Who performs the mock wedding ceremony between Rosalind and Orlando?

3. How long does Orlando say he will be gone before he returns to Rosalind?

4. What excuse does Orlando give for leaving?

5. What question does Jaques ask the Lords he meets in the forest?

6. What did Orlando ask Oliver to bring to Ganymede?

7. Which two animals threatened Oliver while he slept beneath a tree?

8. What wound did Orlando receive while defending his brother?

9. What is Rosalind's response when she hears that Orlando has been injured?

10. Where does Rosalind say she would like to be after she recovers?

Answers

1. Rosalind, as Ganymede, tells Orlando that his Rosalind "would not kill a fly."

2. Celia performs the mock wedding ceremony.

3. Orlando says he will be gone for two hours.

4. Orlando tells Rosalind he must leave to "attend the Duke at dinner."

5. Jaques asks the Lords which of them has killed the deer they are bearing to the Duke.

6. Orlando asked Oliver to bring Ganymede a handkerchief soaked with his blood.

7. Oliver was threatened by a "green and gilded snake" and a lioness.

8. Orlando had flesh torn away on his arm while battling the lioness.

9. When Rosalind learns that Orlando has been injured, she faints.

10. When she regains consciousness, Rosalind comments, "I would I were at home."

Suggested Essay Topics

1. Examine the ways that Rosalind tests Orlando's love for her in Act IV, Scene 1.

2. Explore the ways in which what we have already learned about Orlando foreshadows his courageous actions in saving his brother's life.

3. Discuss the ways that Rosalind's Ganymede disguise proves an advantage and a disadvantage in Act IV, Scenes 1 and 3.

4. Contrast the changing roles of Celia and Oliver in the fourth act with their characterizations earlier in the play.

Act V

Act V, Scene 1

New Character:

William: *a simpleminded young man*

Summary

Touchstone asks Audrey to be patient; he assures her that their marriage will indeed take place. Audrey argues that Sir Oliver Martext was good enough to perform the ceremony, but Touchstone disparages the cleric and moves on to another topic, remarking that there is a youth in the forest who "lays claim" to Audrey. However Audrey, interested only in marrying her urbane man of the court, protests that her supposed suitor "hath no interest in me in the world."

William, an unsophisticated young man of twenty-five, enters. As soon as Touchstone sees his potential rival, he decides to have some fun at his expense. He questions William about his background and inquires as to whether he loves Audrey. William replies that he does. Touchstone officiously asks William if he is "learned." When William replies that he is not, Touchstone launches into an absurd flight of rhetoric that "proves" his right to wed Audrey. The dumbfounded William fails to comprehend.

Touchstone then asserts his claim to the country goatherd in plainer language. He tells William to abandon his courtship, declaring that if he does not he will kill him a hundred and fifty different way. "Therefore," he concludes, "tremble and depart." To this, Audrey adds her own simple pronouncement: "Do, good William." William meekly agrees and exits. Corin enters immediately afterward and tells Touchstone and Audrey that Ganymede and Aliena are seeking them.

Analysis

William is a genuine rustic, the type of character one might have expected to encounter in a rural setting in Shakespeare's time. He stands in sharp contrast to Silvius, a poetic shepherd drawn not from life but from the conventions of pastoral romance. Touchstone deceives the unlearned William, just as he has fooled Audrey, with his displays of "erudition." There is a comic contrast in the polite way that William addresses Touchstone and Touchstone's condescending tone when speaking to his rustic "rival." William uses the polite "you" when speaking to Touchstone, but Touchstone employs a patronizing "thou" in speaking to one whom he considers his inferior. Touchstone's threats, of course, are not to be taken seriously, and his aggressive manner disappears as soon as William exits.

Act V, Scenes 2 and 3

Summary

Orlando has learned that Oliver has fallen in love with Aliena at first sight. He is incredulous at the news, but Oliver assures his brother that his love is genuine and asks for his permission to marry. He tells Orlando that after he is married he plans to give him their father's house "and all the revenue that was old Sir Rowland's." Furthermore, Oliver plans to "here live and die a shepherd." Orlando grants his consent. He tells Oliver that the wedding will take place the next day and bids him to invite the Duke and his followers.

Rosalind enters, still disguised as Ganymede. After she exchanges greetings with Oliver he departs. She tells Orlando that she had been distressed to hear of the wounds he suffered in his battle with the lioness, but Orlando is more worried about his

romantic affairs. Rosalind remarks upon Oliver and Aliena's love for each other and predicts a happy marriage. Orlando replies that he is sad to "look into happiness through another man's eyes," for his own romantic situation seems far less promising.

Rosalind asks if she couldn't again serve as Orlando's Rosalind on the day of the wedding. But Orlando answers that he can "no longer live by thinking." Rosalind assures him that she has a solution to his problem. Since the age of three, she comments, she has "conversed with a magician" who has taught her the secrets of his art. She promises that when Oliver marries Aliena, Orlando will marry his Rosalind as well. She pledges to produce the real Rosalind the next day. Orlando is skeptical, but Ganymede reaffirms "his" promise and tells Orlando to dress in his best clothes and invite his friends to his own wedding.

Silvius and Phebe enter, and Phebe promptly criticizes Ganymede for showing her letter to Silvius. Rosalind tells her that it was her intention to be "despiteful and ungentle." She remarks that Silvius is a faithful shepherd and tells Phebe to love him, for he worships her. Silvius again declares his love for Phebe, but the shepherdess protests that she is in love with Ganymede. Orlando then proclaims his love for Rosalind. With Phebe's infatuation in mind, Rosalind announces that she is "for no woman." The lovers repeat their declarations until finally Rosalind wearies of their sighing: "Pray you, no more of this; 'tis like the howling of Irish wolves against the moon." She pledges to help Silvius if she can; she tells Phebe that she would love her if she could and requests a meeting the next day, promising, "I will marry you if ever I marry a woman, and I'll be married tomorrow." To Orlando, she remarks that she will satisfy him if ever she satisfied a man; she assures him that he will be married the next day. She also promises Silvius that he will be married at the same time.

In Scene 3, Touchstone announces to Audrey that they, too, will be married on the morrow. Two Pages enter, and Touchstone requests a song. The Pages respond by singing "It was a Lover and his Lass," a merry song that celebrates love, marriage, and the pastoral life. When the Pages have finished, Touchstone criticizes the song and their singing: "I count it but time lost to hear such a foolish song. God b' wi' you, and God mend your voices."

Analysis

The notion of love at first sight again appears in Oliver's love for Aliena. In Lodge's *Rosalynde*, Aliena fell in love only after the hero's older brother had rescued her from a gang of thieves. Here we have what seems like an obligatory pairing; even Orlando asks wonderingly, "Is't possible?" However it is also a union with a number of precedents. Rosalind and Orlando also fell in love at first sight, and Phebe became similarly enchanted at her first encounter with Ganymede.

The comic confusion resulting from Rosalind's disguise reaches a climax in Scene 2. Much of the humor in this scene lies in repetition. Each of the lovers reprises his or her declaration of love until finally Rosalind wearies of their "howling" and promises a solution to everyone's problems. She has enjoyed the opportunity to have a last bit of fun with her masculine identity, but now she knows that the masquerade must end the next day.

Note the contrast between "It was a Lover and his Lass" in Scene 3 and Amiens's songs in the second act. Here there are no allusions to winter and rough weather; it is a song of spring and young love, with subtle evocations of the theme of time. This song sets the tone for the wedding scene that follows; each lover will be paired with his lass in joyous finale.

Act V, Scene 4

New Characters:

Hymen: *the god of marriage*

Jaques de Boys: *second son of the late Sir Rowland de Boys; brother of Oliver and Orlando*

Summary

The next day, Duke Senior, Amiens, Jaques, Orlando, Oliver, and Aliena gather in the forest. Duke Senior asks Orlando whether he feels Ganymede can do all he has promised. Orlando replies that he has been wavering between belief and disbelief; he is afraid of being disappointed. Rosalind, still disguised as Ganymede, enters with Silvius and Phebe and asks those who have assembled to have patience while she confirms that everyone has agreed to keep their promises. Duke Senior pledges his permission for Rosalind to marry Orlando if Rosalind appears. Orlando declares that he will marry Rosalind. Phebe says she will marry Ganymede if "he" is willing, but she promises if for any reason she decides not to marry Ganymede she will marry Silvius, who quickly agrees to marry Phebe if she will have him. Rosalind reaffirms her pledge to solve everyone's problems. After cautioning the lovers to "keep your word," she exits with Aliena. Duke Senior remarks that "I do remember in this shepherd boy/ Some lively touches of my daughter's favor." Orlando comments to the Duke that the first time he saw Ganymede he thought "he" was "a brother to your daughter." However he insists that Ganymede is "forest-born."

Touchstone and Audrey enter, and Jaques observes that there seems to be a flood in store, for couples are arriving two by two as they did when the Biblical Noah built his ark. Touchstone and Audrey, he remarks, seem "a pair of very strange beasts, which in all tongues are known as fools." Jaques tells Duke Senior that Touchstone has claimed to have been a courtier. Touchstone immediately retorts that if anyone doubts his word, they may put him to the test. At Jaques' prodding, he launches into witty discourses on the habits of courtiers, their quarrelsome natures, and the seven types of lies they practice. Duke Senior, pleased with Touchstone's wit, agrees with Jaques' observation that Touchstone is "a rare fellow."

Rosalind and Celia, now dressed in feminine attire, enter along with Hymen, the god of marriage. Soft music is heard, and Hymen asks Duke Senior to receive his daughter. Rosalind gives herself, in turn, to her father and to Orlando, and Phebe comments that "If sight and shape be true,/ Why then, my love adieu!" Hymen remarks that confusion has now been brought to an end, and that it is time to "make conclusion/ Of these most strange events." The four pairs of lovers join hands, and Hymen blesses their union. A joyous wedding song follows. Duke Senior welcomes Celia, and Phebe pledges herself to Silvius.

The wedding festivities are interrupted by the sudden entrance of Jaques de Boys, the second son of the late Sir Rowland. He brings the news that Duke Frederick, having learned that every day "men of great worth" were fleeing into the forest of Arden, had raised an army and headed toward the forest with the intention of killing Duke Senior. When Duke Frederick arrived on the outskirts of the forest, however, he met an old religious hermit. After speaking with the hermit, Duke Frederick decided to abandon his deadly mission and forsake the world for a religious life. He also restored his dukedom to his banished brother.

Duke Senior is overjoyed at this news. He welcomes Jaques de Boys and remarks that he has brought additional happiness to his brothers' wedding. He pledges to restore to Oliver the lands Duke Frederick had confiscated, and he names Orlando as his heir. He also promises that the courtiers who have joined him in his exile will share in his good fortune when he returns to his dukedom. He calls for music and a wedding dance.

Only Jaques does not share in the festive spirit. He tells Duke Senior that he plans to join Duke Frederick in an austere religious life, remarking that "Out of these convertites/ There is much matter to be heard and learned." Jaques bestows his blessings upon Duke Senior, Orlando, Oliver, and Silvius, but he cautions Touchstone that his marriage to Audrey is likely to last only two months. He announces his intention to leave the wedding festivities, commenting, "I am for other than for dancing measures." Duke Senior pleads for Jaques to remain, but Jaques refuses, telling the Duke he will find a home in Duke Senior's abandoned cave. He exits, and Duke Senior gives the instruction for the couples to begin their joyous wedding dance.

Analysis

In spite of Orlando's skepticism at the beginning of the scene, everything is happily resolved. While waiting for Rosalind's inevitable entrance, this time in feminine clothes, we are treated to one last debate on the virtues of city life versus country life. Touchstone wittily describes the affectations one might encounter at court: flattery, craftiness, expensive clothing, quarreling. The quarrels he depicts are governed by set rules; the same holds true for the degrees of the lies told by courtiers.

Critics differ in their views of Touchstone in this scene. Some commentators feel that his vein is still satirical: he parodies the language of the affected courtier and burlesques a courtly due. Other critics are of the opinion that Touchstone's remarks are ironic, and that he is clearly "putting on airs." In Act I, Scene 2, Rosalind called Touchstone "Nature's natural," but some observers feel that life in the forest has transformed this witty fool; he is no longer a critic of courtly manners, but rather their staunch defender. Either way, Touchstone's extended flights of rhetoric serve a practical dramatic purpose: they give Ganymede and Aliena time to change their costumes and emerge once again as Rosalind and Celia.

In classical mythology, Hymen was the god of marriage. The name of the god symbolizes the impending consummation of the marriages that will take place. Here, it is interesting to note that in ancient Greek dramas, plays were often resolved by what we known as a *deus ex machina*, literally, a "god from the machine." When mortals were unable to solve their problems, a god was lowered to the stage at a climactic moment to resolve the action—a convention Shakespeare would have been aware of. In this instance, however, the god does not solve the problems of the lovers but merely solemnizes their wedding festivities. Those onstage might well assume that Hymen represents the "magic" that Ganymede has promised; indeed, we are told that "Hymen from heaven" has brought Rosalind. But the audience (or the reader) is aware that it is Rosalind, rather than Hymen, who has brought an end to the "confusion."

With the entrance of Hymen, the play becomes a masque—a popular court entertainment in Shakespeare's time. Masques were usually characterized by music, dancing, and the appearance of supernatural or mythological personages. They featured far less plot than a play, and much of their impact was visual. Generally speaking, masques were allegorical in nature and took as their theme an idealized vision of the power of the reigning monarch and the ruler's divine right to govern. The masque of Hymen serves much the same function. Order has been restored to the proceedings; the chaos brought about when Duke Frederick usurped his brother's dukedom is resolved almost immediately after the wedding song.

In Jaques de Boys' tale of Duke Frederick's encounter with the "old religious man" we see the same type of miraculous conversion we had witnessed earlier in Oliver's transformation. If anything, Duke Frederick's sudden metamorphosis seems more implausible. Still, it is in keeping with the fairy tale nature of much of the play.

There are a number of ironies in the play's resolution. Note that Duke Senior, who has praised the pastoral life, plans a return to the court as soon as the opportunity presents itself. Yet Jaques, who has criticized life in the forest, chooses to remain.

At the end of the play, the caprices of fortune have been corrected; those of good nature have been rewarded, and those who were of evil nature have seen the error of their ways. All are not content, however. Jaques' decision to forego the wedding merrymaking and join Duke Frederick in a religious order lends a jarring note to the festivities, although it is one we might have expected from such a character. Yet his curiosity about Duke Frederick and his new way of life seems genuine, and it is easy to imagine that he well find satisfaction in his company. The ending of the play is by no means completely symmetrical, but the final scene concludes in a joyous spirit of communion and celebration.

Epilogue

Summary

After the wedding dance, Rosalind steps forward and addresses the audience. She comments that a good play needs no epilogue, just as a good wine needs no bush—a reference to the ivy bush vintners in Shakespeare's time used on signs of their trade. Yet she argues that even good plays can be improved with the help of good epilogues. She apologizes for not being a good epilogue, and adds that she cannot slyly gain the audience's approval, for she is not dressed like a beggar; thus, it is improper to plead for an ovation. Instead, she will "conjure" the audience into applause. She addresses the women in the audience, telling them "for the love you bear to men, to like as much of this play that please you." To the men she comments that she hopes the play has pleased them as

well. "If I were a woman," she remarks, "I would kiss as many of you as had beards that pleased me." She adds that she would like as many of the men "as have good beards, or good faces, or sweet breaths" to applaud when she curtsies and exits.

Analysis

In Shakespeare's time, of course, the role of Rosalind was acted by a young man. Rosalind, in expressing the hope that the audience has enjoyed the play, humorously acknowledges this fact. Her reference to conjuring recalls her fanciful tale of being trained by a sorcerer and the "magic" she promises and delivers at the end of the play. Her comments are self-effacing, yet at the same time they appeal to the audience's vanity. If all the women in the audience who liked part of the play and all the men who felt they had "good beards, or good faces, or sweet breaths," responded to her entreaties, she would have been greeted at her exit by a hearty round of applause.

Study Questions

1. How old is William?

2. What does Touchstone threaten to do if William does not relinquish his claim to Audrey?

3. Who does Oliver fall in love with?

4. When does Oliver plan to be married?

5. When does Touchstone tell Audrey they will be married?

6. Who delivers the news of Duke Frederick's conversion?

7. Who was responsible for Duke Frederick's sudden change of heart?

8. Who does Duke Senior name as heir to his newly restored dukedom?

9. What reason does Jaques give for departing the wedding festivities?

10. Who speaks the epilogue of the play?

Answers

1. William tells Touchstone he is twenty-five.

2. Touchstone claims he will kill William "a hundred and fifty ways."

3. Oliver falls in love with Celia in her Aliena disguise.

4. Orlando tells Oliver that the wedding will take place the next day.

5. Touchstone tells Audrey that they, too, will be married the next day.

6. Jaques de Boys, the second son of the late Sir Rowland, delivers the news of Duke Frederick's miraculous conversion.

7. Duke Frederick abandoned his plan to capture and kill his brother after meeting "an old religious man" on the outskirts of the forest.

8. Duke Senior names Orlando as his heir.

9. Jaques tells Duke Senior, "I am for other than for dancing measures."

10. Rosalind speaks the epilogue.

Suggested Essay Topics

1. Compare and contrast the realistically drawn rural characters Corin, William, and Audrey to Silvius and Phebe, who are many ways the conventional "poetic shepherds" of pastoral romance.

2. Explore the ways that Touchstone's behavior differs when he is in the company of "city" and "country" characters.

3. Discuss the role of Jaques in the play and the reasons that may underlie his decision to remain in the forest.

4. Explain the reasons why Duke Senior, after praising the pastoral life, might want to return to the court.

Sample Analytical Paper Topics

The following paper topics are based on the entire play. Following each topic is a thesis and a sample outline. Use these as a starting point for your paper.

Topic #1

Fortune and nature are two of the central themes of William Shakespeare's *As You Like It*. Write an essay that discusses the role of these elements in the lives of Orlando, Oliver, Duke Senior, Duke Frederick, and Rosalind. Nature, in this instance, refers to human nature rather than to the natural world.

Outline

I. Thesis Statement: *Fortune and nature play key roles in the lives of Orlando, Oliver, Duke Senior, Duke Frederick, and Rosalind.*

II. Orlando

    A. Fortune has deprived Orlando of his rightful inheritance.

    B. Fortune enables Orlando to win his wrestling match with Charles and earn the love of Rosalind.

    C. Orlando's relationship with Adam reveals that he is noble by nature.

D. Orlando must leave his home after learning that his brother plans to kill him, but fortune rewards him when he woos and wins Rosalind in the forest.

E. At the end of the play, fortune bestows gifts on the deserving Orlando: he marries the woman he loves and is named heir to a dukedom.

III. Oliver

A. Fortune rewards Oliver with control over his late father's estate.

B. Oliver is revealed by his words and actions as a villain by nature.

C. Fortune prevents Oliver's murderous plots against his brother from succeeding.

D. Oliver encounters ill fortune when his estate is seized by Duke Frederick and he is banished from the court until he finds Orlando.

E. Fortune rewards the undeserving Oliver; Orlando saves his life when he is threatened by a snake and a lioness.

F. Oliver's nature changes after he is rescued by Orlando; he is rewarded by fortune with Celia's love.

IV. Duke Senior

A. Fortune has deprived Duke Senior of the dukedom to which he is the rightful heir.

B. Duke Senior makes the most of his misfortune by establishing a happy life in the Forest of Arden; his optimistic nature enables him to find sweetness in his adversity.

C. Duke Senior reveals by his words and actions that he is generous and kind; for example, he invites Orlando and Adam to share in his feast.

D. Fortune rewards Duke Senior by restoring his dukedom and uniting his daughter in marriage with a man who is also noble in nature.

V. Duke Frederick

    A. Fortune has unfairly rewarded Duke Frederick with a dukedom to which he is not entitled.

    B. Duke Frederick is revealed as a villain by nature; he despises Orlando and Rosalind because they are virtuous and well-liked.

    C. Fortune miraculously thwarts Duke Frederick's plan to capture and kill Duke Senior when he encounters an old religious hermit on the outskirts of the forest.

    D. Duke Frederick, like Oliver, undergoes a sudden change in his nature and renounces his former ways.

VI. Rosalind

    A. Fortune has deprived Rosalind of her father and her status as daughter of the reigning duke; she describes herself as "one out of suits with fortune."

    B. In Rosalind's witty dialogue with Celia in Act 1, Scene 2, she comments that fortune's benefits are "mightily mis-placed," and that the goddess Fortune is, by tradition, blind and bestows her gifts unequally.

    C. Rosalind is revealed as romantic and kind by nature; the people of the dukedom "praise her for her virtues."

    D. The apparent misfortune of Rosalind's banishment is, in fact, a stroke of good fortune, for Orlando has also arrived in the forest; Rosalind is granted the opportunity to test Orlando's love for her while she is disguised as Ganymede.

    E. At the end of the play, fortune rewards Rosalind with a reunion with her father, whose dukedom has been restored, and marriage to the man she loves.

VII. Conclusion: In *As You Like It*, many of the characters have just cause to "rail on Lady Fortune" and the caprices of human nature. By the end of the play, however, those who were of evil nature have changed for the better, and fortune's gifts have been fairly bestowed.

Topic #2

In *As You Like It,* Shakespeare often contrasts city life and country life. The pastoral life is praised by a number of characters in this play, yet Shakespeare suggests frequently that it is not as ideal a life as many of the characters believe. In doing so, Shakespeare also satirizes the conventions of pastoral romance. Write an essay in which you discuss Shakespeare's portrayal of city life and country life in each of the play's five acts.

Outline

I. Thesis Statement: *In* As You Like It, *Shakespeare presents multiple views of city life and country life.*

II. Act I

    A. The court is shown to be a place of corruption and villainy through the actions of Oliver and Duke Frederick.

    B. Courtly manners are satirized as "affected" in the character of Le Beau.

    C. The banished Duke Senior's life in the Forest of Arden is idealized when Charles describes the Duke and his men as fleeting the time carelessly "as they did in the golden world."

    D. Celia comments that she and Rosalind, in leaving the court for the countryside, are going "To liberty, and not to banishment."

III. Act II

    A. Duke Senior praises the virtues of the pastoral life, which is also celebrated in Amiens' songs; life in the forest seems far removed from life at the "envious court."

    B. Jaques comments on the irony of the Duke and his men killing and frightening the animals in the forest, which they have usurped just as Duke Frederick has usurped his brother's dukedom.

    C. Duke Senior and Amiens reveal that country life has its hardships: winter and rough weather.

D. Touchstone comments wryly that "When I was at home, I was in a better place," and Jaques remarks that a man is a fool to "leave his wealth and ease" to live in the forest.

E. Corin remarks that the landowner he serves is "of churlish disposition" and unlikely to get into heaven; unjust behavior is not confined to the city.

F. Adam almost starves to death in the forest, where food isn't readily available.

IV. Act III

A. Touchstone praises some elements of the pastoral life, but he also remarks that it is tedious and austere.

B. Corin extols the virtues of his simple life as a shepherd and makes fun of the formal manner of the court.

C. Orlando remarks on the timelessness of the forest—a departure from the regimentation of the court.

D. Audrey is revealed as a simple, unsophisticated rustic who does not understand Touchstone's witticisms as the "city" characters do.

E. Silvius is disclosed as miserable and comically extreme in his passion, while Phebe is depicted as vain and petulant; Shakespeare satirizes the conventional view of idealized shepherds living in a harmonious pastoral world.

V. Act IV

A. The deer killed by the Forest Lords is another reminder that the pastoral life has its harshnesses.

B. Oliver reveals that the forest can be a dangerous place; wild beasts—a snake and a lioness—lurk as a threat.

VI. Act V

A. The character of William again reveals that the country dwellers are often unsophisticated and "unlearned."

B.   The song sung by the two Pages, with its images of green cornfields and singing birds, celebrates the virtues of a country spring.

C.   Touchstone's speeches about courtly manners and the "rules of quarreling" at court are reminders of the "painted pomp" and affectation of city life.

D.   The forest is shown to be a magical place; Duke Frederick need only arrive at its outskirts to be converted.

E.   Duke Senior, who has praised the pastoral life, decides to return to the city at the first opportunity; only Jaques, a critic of life in the forest, chooses to remain.

VII.   Conclusion: Shakespeare, in *As You Like It*, often seems to be praising the virtues of the pastoral life at the expense of city life, yet ultimately he offers a more balanced view. Both city life and country life are shown to have their advantages and disadvantages.

Topic #3

As You Like It offers a number of differing perspectives on the forms that love can take. These range from love at first sight (with resulting complications) to unrequited passion to frank desire to satisfy one's physical needs. Write an essay that describes and analyzes the courtships of the four couples who are married at the end of the play.

Outline

I.   Thesis Statement: *In his depiction of the four couples—Orlando and Rosalind, Silvius and Phebe, Oliver and Celia, and Touchstone and Audrey—Shakespeare offers four differing perspectives on love and its many aspects.*

II.   Orlando and Rosalind

A.   Rosalind falls in love with Orlando at first sight at the wrestling match.

B. Orlando falls in love with Rosalind at first sight but he is speechless to thank her when she gives him a chain as a reward for his victory.

C. Orlando expresses his love for Rosalind by writing poems to her and carving her name on trees.

D. Rosalind panics when she learns Orlando is in the Forest of Arden and wonders how her Ganymede disguise might complicate matters, but she turns her disguise into a advantage when she decides to test the extent of Orlando's love for her.

E. In her conversations with Orlando while she is in disguise, Rosalind punctures Orlando's conventional notions of how a lover should act; she gets him to adopt a realistic attitude toward the woman he loves.

F. Orlando proves to the disguised Rosalind that he is truly in love, and Rosalind realizes how deeply she loves Orlando, thus allowing Rosalind to abandon her disguise and marry him.

III. Silvius and Phebe

A. Silvius' love for Phebe is unrequited, leaving him in agony.

B. Phebe, a "poetic shepherdess," is disdainful of Silvius, spurning his advances.

C. Silvius uses the conventional language of love; like Orlando he claims he will die if the woman he is obsessed with does not love him.

D. Rosalind chastises Phebe for her pride, but Phebe falls in love with Rosalind in her Ganymede disguise.

E. Phebe, now in love with Ganymede, is more charitable toward Silvius, but she deceives him by making him deliver a poetic love letter.

F. Rosalind employs a ruse to bring Silvius and Phebe together; her folly exposed, Phebe falls in love with Silvius and agrees to marry the shepherd who adores her.

IV. Oliver and Celia

A. Celia, perhaps feeling left out after her best friend has fallen in love with Orlando, takes the lead in questioning a stranger who arrives in the forest.

B. Oliver, having learned to love his brother after years of hatred and resentment, tells Orlando that he has fallen in love with Aliena.

C. Orlando is incredulous that his brother has fallen in love at first sight, but he realizes his brother is sincere in his affections.

D. The love of Oliver and Celia seems as sudden as Oliver's "miracuous" conversion, but it is in keeping with the play's conventions; Orlando and Rosalind also fell in love at first sight and Phebe had the same experience when she met Ganymede.

V. Touchstone and Audrey

A. Touchstone and Audrey are an odd couple from the first; the unsophisticated Audrey does not understand Touchstone's witticisms.

B. Touchstone is certain that Audrey will make him a cuckold after they are married, but he still resolves to marry her.

C. Touchstone confesses candidly to Jaques that he is marrying Audrey because "man hath his desires."

D. Touchstone want Sir Oliver Martext to perform the wedding ceremony because the marriage might not be legal, thus leaving him free to eventually abandon his wife.

E. Touchstone deliberately puts off the marriage, but when William appears, Touchstone asserts his claim to Audrey, who has eyes only for her sophisticated "man of the court."

F. At the wedding festivities, Jaques predicts that Touchstone and Audrey's marriage will last only two months.

VI. Conclusion In *As You Like It*, Shakespeare provides a comic glimpse at the foibles of love through the disparate romantic experiences of four couples. Three of the marriages at the end of the play promise to be happy ones, yet the fourth is unlikely to last.

Topic #4

Role playing is one of the central themes of *As You Like It*. Jaques remarks that "one man in his time plays many parts" and the action of the play reveals this to be true. *As You Like It* also contains a number of additional theatrical analogies. For example, Duke Senior remarks that "This wide and universal theatre/ Presents more woeful pageants that the scene/ Wherein we play in." Later, Corin invites Rosalind and Celia to witness a "pageant truly played" in Silvius' courtship of Phebe, and Rosalind replies, "I'll prove a busy actor in their play." Write an essay in which you discuss the character of Rosalind and the many roles she plays.

Outline

I. Thesis Statement: *Jaques' observation that "one man in his time plays many parts" is particularly appropriate in the case of Rosalind, the main character of the play.*

II. Rosalind's role at court

   A. The royal princess lamenting for her banished father.

   B. The loyal friend to her cousin Celia.

   C. The young woman falling in love with an attractive young man after his heroic victory.

III. Decision to adopt the role of Ganymede

   A. Rosalind comments on the disparity between "a hidden woman's fear" and the "swashing and maritial outside" of the disguise she will adopt.

   B. Rosalind's new role is necessary to assure her safety (and Celia's) in the countryside.

IV. Arrival in the forest

    A. Rosalind, now disguised as Ganymede and weary after her journey, comments that she could find it in her heart to "disgrace my apparel and cry like a woman"; she will continue to play the role of a woman to those aware of her true identity.

    B. Rosalind's disguise as Ganymede passes its first test when Corin calls her "gentle sir"; she plays the role of a young man to those unaware of her disguise.

V. Act III, Scenes 2, 3, and 5

    A. Rosalind responds to Orlando's presence in the forest like a woman, and she wonders what to do with her doublet and hose; when she is with Celia she plays a woman in love.

    B. Rosalind decides to "play the saucy lackey" when Orlando enters, using her disguise to her advantage.

    C. Rosalind pledges to play the role of "psychologist/physician" to cure Orlando of his lovesickness.

    D. Rosalind attempts to play the role of matchmaker with Silvius and Phebe, but her efforts backfire when Phebe falls in love with Ganymede.

VI. Act IV, Scenes 1 and 3

    A. Rosalind, as Ganymede, confidently plays Rosalind for Orlando; she first plays "Rosalind" as a skeptic.

    B. Ganymede then plays a second Rosalind, this time in a more receptive mood.

    C. Ganymede plays the role of a bride in the mock marriage ceremony while Celia plays the priest.

    D. Rosalind again plays matchmaker for Silvius and Phebe.

    E. Ganymede reacts as a woman at the sight of Orlando's blood; she faints and makes the excuse to Oliver that it was a result of playing a woman's role too well.

VIII. Act V, Scenes 2 and 4; Epilogue

    A. Rosalind promises to play the role of a sorceress to solve Orlando's problems.

    B. Rosalind again plays the role of matchmaker/problem solver for Silvius, Phebe, and Orlando.

    C. With everyone's problems solved, Rosalind realizes her male role is no longer necessary and resumes her female role.

    D. Rosalind adopts new roles as both crown princess and wife at the end of Scene 4.

    E. Rosalind drops character in the Epilogue to admit what Shakespeare's audience knew all along; "she" is now a male actor who has played the role of a woman impersonating a man.

IX. Conclusion: In keeping with the many theatrical analogies in *As You Like It*, the character of Rosalind does indeed "play many parts."

Topic #5

Time is one of the many themes in William Shakespeare's *As You Like It*. Write an essay in which you explore Shakespeare's references to time in the play.

Outline

I. Thesis Statement: *In As* You Like It, *Shakespeare explores the theme of time in many different ways.*

II. Act I

    A. We learn that Duke Senior and his court-in-exile "fleet the time carelessly as they did in the golden world."

    B. Court life seems far more regimented than the description of life in the forest.

III. Act II

   A. Adam's faithful nature is underscored by the fact that he has served the household of Sir Rowland de Boys from the age of seventeen "till now almost fourscore."

   B. We hear that Touchstone withdrew a sundial from his pocket and commented comically on time, and that Jaques laughed an hour by his dial.

   C. Orlando comments that the Duke and his followers "lose and neglect the creeping hours of time."

   D. Amiens' songs evoke the changing of the seasons.

   E. Jaques' "Seven Ages of Man" speech charts man's progress from infancy to death.

IV. Act III

   A. Duke Frederick commands Oliver to find Orlando within a year or he will forfeit his lands and goods.

   B. One of Orlando's poems, read by Celia, comments, "How brief the life of man."

   C. Orlando remarks to Ganymede that "There's no clock in the forest," and Rosalind replies that true lovers are prompt.

   D. Rosalind comments that "Time travels in diverse paces with diverse persons" and gives several examples.

V. Act IV

   A. Orlando, careless about time, arrives nearly an hour late for his meeting with Ganymede.

   B. Rosalind again reminds Orlando that true lovers arrive on time and chides him for being as slow as a snail; she warns him that his next lateness will be his last.

   C. Rosalind tells Orlando that the world is six thousand years old and in that time no one has ever died for love; she tells him to be realistic and asks him not to promise he will love her "for ever and a day."

    D. Orlando promises to return in two hours, and Rosalind cautions him to be on time.

    E. Orlando is again late for his appointment, setting up potential complications, but this time he has a good excuse.

VI. Act V

    A. Touchstone has delayed his marriage to Audrey but tells her "we shall find a time."

    B. Oliver, like Orlando, Rosalind, and Phebe, falls in love in an instant.

    C. The song sung by the two Pages contains references to time, and Touchstone comments that the moment he spent listening to it was "time lost."

    D. Jaques predicts that the marriage of Touchstone and Audrey will last only two months.

VII. Conclusion: The theme of time, present throughout the play, has both serious and comic implications. In the end, time has healed all wounds, and most of the principal characters look forward to a happy future.

SECTION EIGHT

Bibliography

Barber, C. L. *Shakespeare's Festive Comedy*. Princeton: Princeton University Press, 1959.

Bloom, Harold, ed. *Major Literary Characters: Rosalind*. New York: Chelsea House, 1992.

Bloom, Harold, ed. *Modern Critical Interpretation: William Shakespeare's As You Like It*. New York: Chelsea House, 1988.

Campbell, Oscar James and Edward G. Quinn, eds. *The Reader's Encyclopedia of Shakespeare*. New York: Crowell, 1966.

Derrick, Patti S. "Rosalind and the Nineteenth-Century Woman: Four Stage Interpretations." *Theatre Survey* 26 (November 1985), 143-162.

French, Marilyn. *Shakespeare's Division of Experience*. New York: Summit Books, 1981.

Grebanier, Bernard. *Then Came Each Actor.* New York: David McKay, 1975.

Halio, Jay L. and Barbara C. Millard. *As You Like It: An Annotated Bibliography*, 1940-1980. New York: Garland, 1985.

Kott, Jan. *Shakespeare Our Contemporary*. Trans. Boleslaw Taborski. Rev. ed. Garden City, NY: Anchor Books, 1966.

McFarland, Thomas. *Shakespeare's Pastoral Comedy*. Chapel Hill: University of North Carolina Press, 1972.

Odell, G. C. D. *Shakespeare from Betterton to Irving*. 2 vols. New York: Scribner's, 1920.

Parrott, Thomas M. *Shakespearean Comedy*. New York: Russell & Russell, 1962.

Partridge, Eric. *Shakespeare's Bawdy*. Rev. ed. New York: Dutton, 1969.

Reynolds, Peter. *Penguin Critical Studies: As You Like It*. London: Penguin, 1988.

Shakespeare, William. *As You Like It*. London: Penguin Books, 1981.

Shaw, John. "Fortune and Nature in 'As You Like It.'" *Shakespeare Quarterly* 6 (1955), 45-50.

Speaight, Robert. *Shakespeare On the Stage*. Boston: Little, Brown, 1973.

Ward, John Powell. *Twayne's New Critical Introductions to Shakespeare: As You Like It*. New York: Twayne, 1992.

Wilson, Edwin, ed. *Shaw on Shakespeare*. New York: Dutton, 1961.

Wilson, John Dover. *Shakespeare's Happy Comedies*. Evanston, Il: Northwestern University Press, 1962.

MAXnotes

REA's Literature Study Guide

MAXnotes® are student-friendly. They offer a fresh look at masterpieces of literature, sented in a lively and interesting fashion. **MAXnotes®** offer the essentials of what should know about the work, including outlines, explanations and discussions of the p character lists, analyses, and historical context. **MAXnotes®** are designed to help you t independently about literary works by raising various issues and thought-provoking ideas questions. Written by literary experts who currently teach the subject, **MAXnotes®** enha your understanding and enjoyment of the work.

Available **MAXnotes®** include the following:

RESEARCH & EDUCATION ASSOCIATION
61 Ethel Road W. • Piscataway, New Jersey 08854
Phone: (908) 819-8880

Please send me more information about MAXnotes®.

Name _____

Address _____

City _____ State _____ Zip _____

The High School Tutor

The **HIGH SCHOOL TUTORS** series is based on the same principle as the n comprehensive **PROBLEM SOLVERS**, but is specifically designed to meet the need high school students. REA has recently revised all the books in this series to include expar review sections, new material, and newly-designed covers. This makes the books even n effective in helping students to cope with these difficult high school subjects.